Ⓣ **Tetra**

TERRAFAUNA®

Digest for the Successful Terrarium

by Richard D. Bartlett

Learn how to establish and maintain
a successful terrarium —
semi-aquatic, aquatic, dry-land — or pond.

The Green Iguana, *Iguana iguana* ssp., a popular dry-land terrarium reptile, loves the petals of fresh flowers. *Photo*: Ruth Sander

Tetra-Terrafauna's
DIGEST FOR THE SUCCESSFUL TERRARIUM
A Tetra Press Publication
By Richard D. Bartlett

©1998 Tetra SecondNature. All Rights Reserved.
A Division of Warner-Lambert
TETRA SECONDNATURE
3001 Commerce Street
Blacksburg, VA 24060
Tel: 1-800-526-0650
Internet: http://www.tetra-fish.com

ISBN: 1-56465-172-X
Library of Congress Catalog #: 89-50849
Tetra Press Item Number: 16040-01

Printed in Hong Kong

Cover photos are: TOP LEFT: Green Tree Python, *Chondropython viridis;* TOP RIGHT: Knight Anole, *Anolis equestris;* BOTTOM LEFT: Baby Turtles; BOTTOM RIGHT: Golden Tree Frog, *Litoria aurea*.

All photos by the author except for the following, which were taken by John Tashjian: all cover photos; San Francisco Garter Snake, p. 6; Caecilian, p. 10; Lesser Siren, p. 11; Surinam Toad, p. 17; Elephant Trunk Snake, p. 20; Painted Turtle, p. 22; Mississippi Map Turtle, p. 23; Barred Tiger Salamander, p. 30; Crocodile Lizard, p. 42; Red-Eyed Tree Frog, p. 47; Broad-Headed Skink, p. 51; Leopard Gecko, p. 54; Collared Lizard, p. 55; Tokay, p. 57; Desert Iguana, p. 57; Green Iguana, p. 61.

A special thanks goes to John Tashjian, who has spent a lifetime photographing herptiles in nature and in captivity throughout the world.

All line drawings by Patricia Bartlett, except for those on pp. 9 and 24, which were done by K. Tscheschner.

Table of Contents

Introduction

In the great and well-ordered scheme of zoological classification, the orders of amphibians and reptiles fall between the fishes and the birds. The study of reptiles and amphibians is termed "herpetology," and those who study these animals, "herpetologists." This latter term is often preceded by either the word "amateur" or "professional." It is an intriguing field, with a sizeable contingent of dedicated followers.

Like most fishes and birds, a great many amphibians and reptiles will not only lead long lives in captivity, but may be induced to breed as well. For those among us who induce and promote the captive breeding of reptiles and amphibians, a new word has been coined: "herpetoculturist." I hope that you will see this term with ever-increasing frequency, for with the acceptance of herpetoculture and the dedication of herpetoculturists, fewer and fewer specimens need be taken from the wild to satisfy hobbyists' demands. We ask that you support both our efforts and conservation practices by insisting whenever possible on captive-bred specimens. Doing so also has a hidden benefit for you, the purchaser. By insisting on captive-bred reptiles and amphibians you are more or less assured of acquiring parasite- and disease-free specimens that feed readily.

Homes for your herptiles, whether of simple hammer-and-saw construction, elaborate, precise cabinetry, or merely converted aquaria, are usually referred to as "terraria" ("terrarium" in the singular). Aquaria are often the most suitable, for they are both waterproof and draft-proof, are readily available, and all manner of accessories, such as lighting and tops, may be obtained for them with equal ease.

A terrarium made from a converted aquarium may be of virtually any size, be it standard or custom-made. As with aquaria, smaller means neither better nor easier. In fact, the larger the land or water mass of your enclosure, the more forgiving it will be of minor mistakes or oversights. You should attempt to tailor the enclosure to the lifestyles of the creatures you wish to maintain. Terrestrial reptiles and amphibians would wish the greatest amount of floor space practicable. Arboreal species would feel more at home in a proportionately tall enclosure with branches and hiding areas secured at various levels. Predominantly aquatic species require a greater volume of water than would landlubbers of similar size. And provide ALL terraria with escape-proof covers!

A periodic and thorough cleansing of your terrarium is necessary. However, after cleaning, a rinsing and drying prior to the reintroduction of your inhabitants is equally important. Some household cleaners may be irritating or fatal to your specimens. Cleaning solutions that contain phenols (such as Pine-Sol) should NEVER be used. Conversely, most herptiles are rather tolerant of disinfectants and cleaning agents containing chlorine and alcohol. But remember, RINSE, VENTILATE, and DRY your terrarium before replacing your specimens.

It is best to learn as much as you can about the natural history of each species of amphibian or reptile that you intend to keep. For you, the keeper, to assume a generality may prove fatal to your specimens. For instance, it is folly to believe that all species originating from those areas that we term "the tropics" do, indeed, appreciate tropical temperatures. Many such species are

A Bog Turtle, *Clemmys muhlenbergi,* emerging from its burrow in a terrarium.

partial to the coolness of mountain elevations. While they may require a "hot spot" for basking, their health will quickly deteriorate if they are maintained perpetually warm. Not all desert species desire absolute dryness. Many dwell in comparatively humid riparian habitats. Others may be so adapted to the low relative humidity of desert conditions that they are unable to adapt to areas of high humidity. Conversely, while the experience is seldom fatal, species transported from humid to arid areas may have difficulty in shedding their skins or completing other necessary functions. While some species will be unable to breed unless provided with a period of dormancy, others may succumb if so subjected. Read! Learn! Exchange information and ideas!

Unfortunately, the knowledge of how to maintain and breed reptiles and amphibians has been relatively slow in its accumulation, and even slower in its dissemination. It is only within the last few years that books and products to assist the herpetological hobbyist have begun to appear regularly in pet shops. To adequately address captive propagation of individual species (a discipline in itself) would require far more space than I have been allotted here. However, I will make brief mention of some of the techniques currently in use:

1. The alteration of photoperiod (the number of daylight hours versus those of darkness) is deemed beneficial. Natural seems best.
2. Those species from temperate climates or high altitudes seem to benefit from a lengthy period of "hibernation." Cooling and keeping them in darkness for a period of about three months

seems to yield the best results.

3. Tropical species, while often having no true period of hibernation or radical seasonal alteration of day length, may still be stimulated by the seasons—the wet versus the dry. Misting a cage gently with an atomizer once or twice daily (especially during the evening hours) may successfully induce breeding.

4. Simultaneously using two males to a single female may induce a series of responses that will ultimately culminate in the dominant male breeding the female. Depending on the species, the males may fight savagely. Be ready to intercede if necessary.

5. Luteinizing and releasing hormones (LH-RH) are often used to induce ovulation and spermatogenesis in properly cycled amphibia.

I will, within this book, touch on most of the basics necessary to the successful keeping of the several terrarium/cage types. I also mention several reptile and amphibian species well adapted for life in each. However, it is neither possible, nor intended, that the information within these few pages be considered comprehensive. Listed on page 76 are the titles of several longer, hence more complete, guides. Among these are some that will enumerate and identify diseases and their treatments, discuss the raising of the live foods so desired by most herptiles, document adventures with reptiles and amphibians in the field, and give general guidelines for breeding your captives.

San Francisco Garter Snake,
Thamnophis sirtalis tetrataenia.

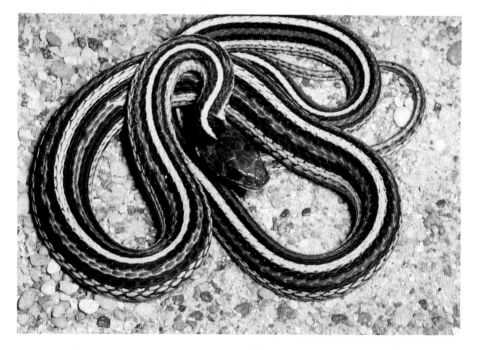

6

Glossary of Terms

Ambient temperature: The temperature of the environment which surrounds the mentioned specimen.

Anterior: Pertaining to the front or head end.

Anterioventral: Pertaining to the front of the lower surface.

Aquatic: Living in the water.

Arboreal: Living or residing in trees or bushes.

Carapace: The upper shell of a turtle.

Crepuscular: Active at dawn and/or dusk.

Cryptic coloration: A concealing or camouflaging color or pattern.

Dewlap: The fan of throat skin displayed by certain lizards; e.g., anoles, iguanas, and others.

Dichromatism: Difference of color between individuals of the same species. May be sex-linked.

Dimorphism: Difference of color, form, or otherwise between individuals of the same species; often sex-linked.

Diurnal: Active by day.

Dorsal: Pertaining to the upper surface.

Dorsolateral: Pertaining to the upper sides.

Dorsolateral ridge/dorsolateral fold: A glandular ridge that appears dorsolaterally on certain frog species.

Dorsum: The upper surface.

Ectotherm/ectothermic: An animal which regulates its body temperature by utilizing behavioral means and outside stimuli (such as basking, etc.). Reptiles and amphibians are ectotherms. Old term: "cold-blooded."

Endemic: Confined, restricted, or indigenous to a specific area or region.

Fernery: A terrarium, cage, or other enclosure in which ferns are the predominant growth.

Genus: A grouping of related kinds (species).

Hybrid: The offspring that results from the breeding of a female of one species by a male of another.

Lateral: Pertaining to the side.

Metamorphosis: The transformation from the larval to the adult stage.

Middorsal: Pertaining to the middle of the back.

Midventral: Pertaining to the middle of the belly.

Monotypic: A group (such as a genus) represented by a single kind.

Neoteny/neotenic: Achieving sexual maturity while in larval form (a characteristic of certain aquatic or semi-aquatic salamanders).

Nocturnal: Active at night.

Plastron: The lower shell of a turtle.

Posterior: Pertaining to the rear.

Posterioventral: Pertaining to the rear portion of the lower surface.

Race: Subspecies.

Semi-aquatic: Capable of living (or preferring to live) on land and water. Pond turtles and most true frogs are examples.

Species: One or more related forms that, together, constitute a genus. Abbreviation: sp.

Subspecies: A subdivision of a species, such as a race or variety. Abbreviation: ssp.

Terrestrial: Dwelling on land.

Taxonomy: The science of classifying plants and animals.

Ventral: Pertaining to the lower surface.

Note: All temperatures are given in degrees Fahrenheit.

7

Aquatic Terrarium (Aquarium)

Aquaria are now commonplace in both home and office. Maintenance products such as filters, pumps, and water conditioners have become so perfected and "how to" books so detailed that virtually any person with the desire to have an aquarium will be able to succeed in his or her endeavors. While many hobbyists think only of fish when the word "aquarium" is mentioned, there are available in your pet shop many amphibians, and a few reptiles, that thrive in such aquatic environments.

Rather than delve into the details of setting up an aquarium, I refer you to the Tetra Press booklet *Digest for the Successful Aquarium*. Note, however, that a tropical, aquatic terrarium will require a heater; a submersible aquarium type is recommended, since it effectively heats both the water AND the atmosphere above. Be sure to select the correct wattage for the amount of water to be heated. The most commonly kept amphibians will thrive at room temperature, especially in a centrally heated home.

The tank substrate should consist of well-washed aquarium gravel. A filter is also essential, and the efficient and highly flexible Tetra foam cartridge system is excellent for this purpose. This system provides both biological and mechanical filtration, and operates from a standard aquarium air pump. The aquatic terrarium should have a background which is beneficial, not only for aesthetic reasons but also to provide the herptile with a sense of security. The interior decor will be dictated by the size and type of the creatures selected, as well as by your personal taste.

The Tetra Double Brillant Filter.

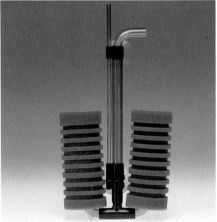

A simple, yet effective, aquarium set-up.

Small amphibians such as the Dwarf Siren, small Caecilians, and small aquatic frogs are entirely compatible with live or artificial plants, and log and driftwood decorations. Larger species, including larger Sirens, Axolotls, and Surinam Toads, may require decorations that are firmly anchored.

Among others, Water Dogs, Hell-benders, Newts, and Clawed Frogs are popular aquatic terrarium residents. While native Water Snakes are not adaptable to a fully aquatic environment, the Elephant Trunk Snake is. Always seek your dealer's advice on herptile compatibility and special environmental requirements. And always handle amphibians very carefully and with moist hands; be sure to wash your hands after handling any herptile.

Always be sure to condition tap water. Many municipalities, and even some urban communities, add purifying agents to their water supplies. While the most common additive is still chlorine, the more complex chloramine is rapidly overtaking it. Either MUST be removed before your specimens, even those that do not breathe by means of

An aquatic terrarium offers an opportunity to maintain interesting creatures. These herptiles are feeding on ReptoMin Floating Food Sticks.

gills, are introduced. Tetra ContraChlorine Plus is effective in neutralizing both of these chemicals.

Please note: While certain species of fish may be successfully integrated with the various amphibians and reptiles, they may fall victim to or victimize the principal inhabitants. Among other things, fish often pick unceasingly at the exposed bushy gill filaments of larval salamanders. Uncomfortable at best, such ministrations may actually prove fatal for these amphibian residents.

The following species are well-suited to the aquatic terrarium.

Aquatic Caecilian
Other name: Rubber Eel
Typhlonectes species

Size: Although members of this genus near, or even exceed, 2 feet in length, most specimens seen in the aquarium trade are less than half that size.
Description: These brownish-gray-to-charcoal amphibians are somewhat vertically compressed anteriorly, but nearly round posteriorly. The eyes are present, but poorly developed, being represented externally by somewhat lighter colored spots. A short, protrusible, tactile tentacle is present posterior to, and on a level below, the nostril. The body is annulated for its entire length, giving the impression to the uninitiated of a gigantic earthworm. Tail very short and rather bluntly rounded. All limbs lacking.

Preferred temperature: Low 70s.
Food: Worms of various types and suitable size, small dead fish, dead adult brine shrimp, and other such animal material. Some specimens may accept certain of the prepared Tetra foods. Experiment.
Care: These are crepuscular and nocturnal creatures which are distressed by brilliant lighting unless provided with ample hiding places. They are entirely at home in aquaria with a thick layer of plant detritus or mulm. They burrow avidly through such media.
Please note: Not all Caecilian species are aquatic. Certain of them are better adapted for moist terraria.

Caecilian, *Ichthyophis kohtaoensis*. Although a terrestrial and more brightly colored species, this Caecilian is similar in form to the aquatic *Typhlonectes* sp.

Greater and Lesser Siren
Other name: Mud Eel
Siren lacertina and *S. intermedia* ssp.
Size: 24 to 36 inches.
Description: These are rather cylindrical, attenuated, eel-like salamanders. They are of dusky coloration and have bushy exposed gills. The small, but functional, forelimbs may be almost hidden by the gills; four toes on front feet; rear limbs are lacking.
Preferred temperature: 68 to 75 degrees.
Food: Worms, small fish, Tetra Tabi-Min®.
Care: While hiding places are necessary, they, and plants, must be firmly anchored. All Sirens are basically nocturnal.

Dwarf Siren, *Pseudobranchus striatus* ssp.

Dwarf Siren
Other name: Dwarf Mud Eel
Pseudobranchus sp.
Size: 5 to 9 inches.
Description: Dusky, but with narrow-to-broad longitudinal stripes. Only three toes on each forelimb. Otherwise like diminutive Lesser or Greater Sirens.

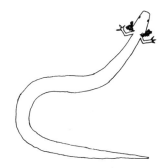

Preferred temperature: 70 to 80 degrees.

Food: White and tubifex worms, chopped earthworms, daphnia, dead baby fish. Some specimens will accept certain of the Tetra brand prepared foods. Experiment.

Care: Hiding places are a must for this interesting but secretive salamander. Most specimens prefer to reside among tangles of aquatic vegetation.

Amphiuma
Other name: Mud Eel
Amphiuma sp.

Size: Adults of the two commonly offered species, the two-toed and the three-toed Amphiumas, often exceed 2 feet in length.

Description: These are the most eel-like of our salamanders. They lack external gills and eyelids, have four tiny, ineffective legs, and are rather cylindrical in cross-section. They, of course, have no fins. Mud or slate gray to charcoal dorsally, lighter ventrally. They have strong jaws and are one of the very few salamander species which resist restraint by biting.

Preferred temperature: 70 to 78 degrees.

Food: Worms, fish, crayfish, certain shellfish, raw meat, and Tetra Reptomin® will be accepted.

Care: Unless supplied with ample hiding places these hardy salamanders will burrow persistently.

Please note: The diminutive and uncommon one-toed Amphiuma, adult at less than a foot in length, is a secretive burrower of muddy northwestern Florida floodplains. It should not be kept in a fully aquatic environment.

Two-Toed Amphiuma, *Amphiuma means.*

Mudpuppies

Other name: Water Dogs
Necturus sp.
Size: From 6 to 16 inches.
Description: The several members of this genus are occasionally available in pet stores. They are typified by a laterally flattened body and head, strongly finned vertically flattened tail, bushy external gills, no eyelids, and only four toes on each of the four feet. Adults are usually muddy colored with a varying degree of spotting or blotching. Juveniles are often longitudinally striped.
Preferred temperature: 68 to 75 degrees.
Food: Worms, small fish, crayfish, raw meat, Tetra ReptoMin. Experiment.
Care: Hiding places, either in the form of bottom snags or submerged plant tangles, are mandatory for long-term success with the Mudpuppies. Excessively warm water may induce the growth of a difficult-to-eradicate skin fungus.

Hellbenders

Cryptobranchus alleganiensis ssp.
Size: Females, the larger sex, often exceed 24 inches in overall length.
Description: In spite of its ever-increasing rarity, small Hellbenders continue to appear on specialty lists and in some of the larger pet shops. They are undoubtedly the most grotesque of the many salamander species. Except for newly hatched young, there are no external gills. The entire animal, except the strongly finned tail, is laterally flattened, an adaptation that enables even large specimens to easily gain seclusion beneath submerged rocks. The dorsal coloration is muddy brown or gray (rarely russet) with sooty spots or blotches. The initial impression when one first sees a Hellbender is of a size-5 salamander in a slimy, size-7 skin . . . the unkempt appearance being enhanced by loose, wavy folds of integument along each side.
Preferred temperature: 65 to 74 degrees.

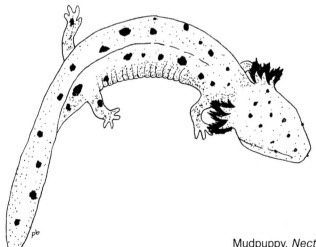

Mudpuppy, *Necturus maculosus* ssp.

13

Food: Although their preferred food is crayfish, Hellbenders will often accept freshly killed fish, worms, mussel and clam strips, and occasionally other types of raw meat.

Care: Hiding places are essential to long-term success with the Hellbender. Excessively warm water often induces the growth of a difficult-to-eradicate skin fungus.

Spotted and Striped Newts
Notopthalmus viridescens ssp. and *N. perstriatus*

Size: To 4½ inches.

Description: These are small, well-proportioned salamanders with angular heads and, when fully adult, prominent tail fins. The dorsum is usually marked with a dual series of black-margined red spots or stripes (these are lacking in the Central Newt). The yellowish belly is peppered with tiny black spots.

Preferred temperature: 68 to 76 degrees.

Food: White and tubifex worms, chopped earthworms, Tetra ReptoMin.

Care: These are undemanding creatures which may be safely maintained with most non-aggressive aquarium fish. Only the larvae and the adults are aquatic. The intermediate stage, often red or reddish in color and known as an "eft," lacks a tail fin and is entirely terrestrial.

Please note: Western Newts of the genus *Taricha* are frequently offered for sale as aquarium animals. In nature, most, like numerous other salamander species, display aquatic propensities only for a few weeks during their breeding seasons. Except for this short duration they are terrestrial creatures of the forest floors. Thus, they are better

Eastern Hellbender, *Cryptobranchus a. alleganiensis.*

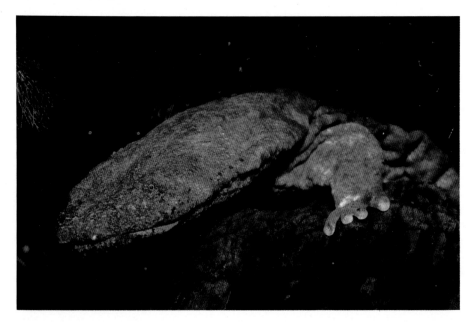

adapted for life in the semi-aquatic terrarium than a fully aquatic environment. Adults may near 6½ inches in length, have brown dorsa and unspotted venters of either yellow or salmon-red.

Axolotls
Other name: Water Dogs
Ambystoma mexicanum and *A. tigrinum* ssp.; more rarely, other species

Size: 6 to 10 inches.
Description: These are big-headed salamanders with prominent, bushy gills and five toes on each hind foot. They are the larvae of the various Mole Salamanders. Except during a short breeding season, most (the Mexican Axolotl is a notable exception) are terrestrial as adults. While the Mexican Axolotl may seldom be induced to metamorphose successfully, others

are likely to be only transient members of the aquarium community, soon graduating to the semi-aquatic terrarium. Those most often offered by pet shops are the juveniles of various Western Tiger Salamanders. Mexican Axolotls, and some others, are capable of attaining sexual maturity while still in the aquatic larval stage. These are said to be neotenic. Axolotls are available in four color phases: albino (white with pink eyes), leucistic (white with black eyes), mottled white and dark, and normal (muddy olive or brown with dark eyes). Aberrant colors of the other species are seldom available.
Preferred temperature: 65 to 75 degrees. Excessively warm or impure water will hasten metamorphosis of those species in which such is possible. When this occurs the gills and tail fin resorb, lungs become functional,

15

Axolotl, *Ambystoma mexicanum*.

and the animal attains other terrestrial characteristics. At this time the water level should be reduced to allow the specimen easier access to the surface. There it will breathe atmospheric oxygen. Drowning is possible at this time. When the gills have been reduced to little more than nubbins the salamander will be ready to take up life in the semi-aquatic or woodland terrarium.

Food: Worms, raw meat, small dead fish, and Tetra ReptoMin will be eagerly accepted. Some larval Ambystomatid Salamanders are known to be predominantly cannibalistic. These would require individual housing.

Care: These interesting creatures are nearly as active by day as by night. Driftwood snags, vegetational tangles, or rocky fissures are appreciated but not mandatory.

Surinam Toad

Pipa pipa (Several other species are known, but this is the one most generally available.)

Size: Commonly attains 8 inches.

Description: This is the most unique-looking of the several commonly offered "underwater" frogs. It is flattened laterally to the point where it looks as if it lost a battle with a steamroller. The head, also flattened, but triangular when viewed from above, is decorated with flaplets of skin at its outer extremities. The eyes are tiny, lidless, and situated dorsally. The forelimbs are directed forward, the fingers terminating in star-shaped tactile organs. The rear legs are muscular and the feet large and strongly webbed. The overall coloration is muddy brown. The mode of reproduction employed by this frog is even stranger than its appearance. Complex aquatic gyrations are performed by the amplexing frogs. During these the large eggs are laid and worked onto the back of the female, where they adhere and become embedded and covered by her glandular integument. Within these pockets of seclusion the eggs hatch and the young develop, finally emerging as tiny replicas of the adults.

Preferred temperature: 72 to 78 degrees.

Food: Worms, small fish, tadpoles, raw meat, and Tetra TabiMin.

Care: Although large, these frogs are secretive, hence prefer driftwood snags and vegetational tangles in which to hide. They are most active at twilight and after darkness falls. Surinam Toads are entirely aquatic and rather helpless when removed from the water.

Surinam Toad, *Pipa pipa*.

Common Underwater Frogs

Other name: Clawed Frogs
Xenopus sp.

Size: Females, somewhat the larger sex, occasionally exceed 4 inches in length.

Description: This species is so regularly available in pet shops that it probably requires no detailed description. Although closely allied to the Surinam Toad, Clawed Frogs are not of such extreme form. They are somewhat flattened. The head is small and surmounted by rather small but protuberant and celestially directed lidless eyes. The forelimbs are directed forward; the fingers have no extraneous tactile organs. The hind legs are muscular, the feet large and fully webbed, and the inner three toes of each hind foot are capped with black, horny claws. Albino (white with pink eyes), leucistic (white with black eyes), and normal (greenish to slate, often with vague blotching, and dark eyes)

Common Clawed Frog, *Xenopus laevis*.

phases are available in the pet trade. The skin is highly glandular and VERY slimy. These are among the most difficult frogs to hand-hold. Use nets.

Preferred temperature: Very undemanding. Between 68 and 80 degrees is acceptable.

Food: Worms, small fish, raw meat, and a wide range of Tetra brand prepared foods are eagerly accepted.

Care: These are among the most easily cared for of the amphibians. They are efficient predators on small fish. Their tanks need to be tightly capped for they are persistent and accomplished in their escape efforts. Snags, caves, and vegetational tangles are appreciated but not mandatory.

Dwarf Underwater Frogs
Other name: Dwarf Clawed Frogs
Hymenochirus sp.

Size: Seldom exceeds 1¼ inches. Females are the larger sex.

Description: These diminutive frogs are quite like the Common Underwater Frog in form, but with a more granular skin and more laterally placed eyes. Although albinos have cropped up, such aberrancy has not yet become established. Normal color is olive green to olive brown.

Preferred temperature: 72 to 80 degrees.

Food: They thrive in the balanced aquarium, eagerly accepting Tetra brand prepared foods. White and tubifex worms are an especial treat.

Care: The tiny size of the Dwarf Underwater Frogs renders them entirely compatible with nearly any non-predaceous aquarium fish.

Oriental Fire-Bellied Toad
Bombina orientalis

Size: Commonly attains 1½ inches.

Description: This is a beautiful species. Dorsally it varies from bright to olive green with an intricate pattern of black reticulations. Ventrally the color is orange-red with black reticulations.

Preferred temperature: 70 to 78 degrees.

Food: In a fully aquatic environment this species is best fed from forceps. It will eagerly accept waxworms, mealworms, small earthworms, small dead fish, and pieces of raw meat.

Care: While not a wholly aquatic species in the strictest sense, this little frog is well adapted to life among mats of floating vegetation. However, if your aquarium does not have a profusion of floating plants such as water sprite, you must provide a piece of floating driftwood or plastic lilypad landing area. This is also an ideal species for the semi-aquatic terrarium.

Please note: The skin secretions of the Fire-Bellied Toad are apt to prove fatal to other amphibian species. Fire-Bellied Toads are best maintained in monotypic groups.

Dwarf Clawed Frog, *Hymenochirus curtipes*.

Oriental Fire-Bellied Toad, *Bombina orientalis*.

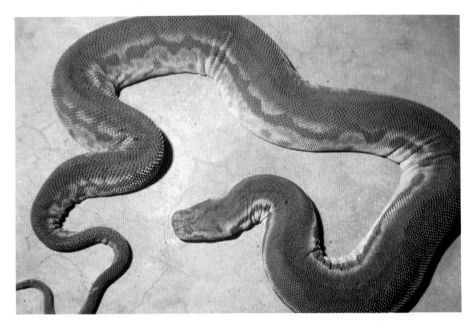

Elephant Trunk Snake, *Acrochordus javanicus*.

Elephant Trunk Snake
Acrochordus javanicus
Size: To more than 6 feet.
Description: This Austral-Asian species is dingy olive, olive brown, or, occasionally, darker. Obscure dark markings are present. The scales are coarse, raspy, and protuberant. There are no enlarged ventral scales. The tongue is proportionately large and deeply bifurcated. When taken from the water the skin of this snake appears several sizes too large. However, in its aquatic habitat it is a well-adapted, graceful creature.
Preferred temperature: 75 to 80 degrees.
Food: The diet seems restricted to fish.
Care: This is one of the very few snakes that are well adapted to life in a fully aquatic environment. Juveniles are often seen in pet shops. They ap-

preciate dark hiding spots, either in the form of rocky cave formations or driftwood snags, and are not at all at home when these are not available. The hiding spots should be firmly anchored. Enough marine salt, or even non-iodized table salt, to produce a vaguely brackish environment will prove beneficial to this species.
Please note: Our native natricine Water Snakes are NOT adapted for a fully aquatic environment. They must be maintained in a manner similar to Rat Snakes or King Snakes (see the chapter entitled "Homes for Herptiles").

Turtle Aquarium

People maintain more baby semi-aquatic turtles in captivity than any other reptile species. Of the many species native to the United States, three, the Red-Eared Slider, *Trachemys scripta elegans,* the several races of Painted Turtle, *Chrysemys picta* ssp., and the Common Map Turtle, *Graptemys geographica,* are the most frequently seen captives. Of these three, the first two are the most tolerant of captive conditions and diets.

In the United States, the sale of turtles with a carapace length of less than four inches is illegal. However, wild baby turtles are still widely kept as pets.

Contrary to popular belief, the worst conditions under which a baby turtle can be kept are those that exist in the so-called turtle bowl. This creates a totally unnatural environment . . . one in which the animals are forced to live in their own filth. When they are kept in such a fashion it is little wonder that most turtles soon sicken and die.

To successfully keep turtles in good health it is necessary to follow several criteria. Most important among these are an aquatic terrarium of adequate size and design, proper illumination for basking, cleanliness, and a nutritious vitamin- and mineral-fortified diet.

Your turtle aquarium should be a minimum of 20 gallons in size. This is of sufficient size for three or four healthy, active, rapidly growing specimens.

Since turtles are both susceptible to and known to transmit diseases (such as salmonellosis), it is important to avoid handling them more than necessary. When it is necessary to do so, wash your hands both before and, most especially, after picking one up.

Red-Eared Slider, *Trachemys scripta elegans.*

Painted Turtle, *Chrysemys picta* ssp.

Most (but NOT all) semi-aquatic turtles are powerful swimmers that are happiest if provided with several inches of clean water. From this water an "island" should protrude on which they may rest, bask, and dry in the warmth of a light. There are several ways to create an island in your turtle aquarium. While a piece of floating styrofoam wedged securely between two glass sides is the simplest, it is not the most aesthetically pleasing. However, should you decide to use this, it should be wedged on a gentle angle, the lower edge being slightly below the water surface to provide an easy access for your specimens. Other alternatives are provided by the prudent use of driftwood, wood blocks, smooth stones, or decorative cork. Be sure that the wood blocks are NOT pressure-treated or painted wood. Whenever possible, it is best if the turtles can have access to the basking island from all four sides and that they be able to ascend easily to its summit. This means that at least one edge must be completely immersed in the water. Your pets will then get exercise both while swimming and while ascending to their basking location.

A turtle aquarium must not be completely filled with water. The water level should be at least three to four inches from the top (a water depth of from six to ten inches is adequate for most). This will enable you to elevate the basking island sufficiently for your turtle to be entirely dry, yet have the island sufficiently below the top of your aquarium to prevent the escape of your pet.

The substrate used in your turtle aquarium can be the same as that used for a fish aquarium. Gravel of small enough size to prevent uneaten food from being lodged in it irretrievably, and also small enough not to crack the aquarium glass as your turtles dig and move it about, is best. Again, if aesthetics are not important, a bare tank bottom would be the easiest to keep clean. The water temperature should be maintained at approximately 77 to 80 degrees.

A filter is extremely important, as turtles are very messy. The Tetra Brillant Filter® with a double cartridge is recommended for aquaria of up to 20 gallons in size. For larger aquaria, multiple Brillant Filters or the Super Brillant Filter can be used. The aquarium water should be changed frequently. This is best done with the Tetra Hydro-Clean, which removes accumulated debris from the gravel as it siphons. Be sure to use ONLY a self-starting Hydro-Clean; starting the siphon using your mouth could cause illness. A 50 to 60 percent weekly water change is recommended to ensure a clean environment.

Mississippi Map Turtle, *Graptemys kohni.*

23

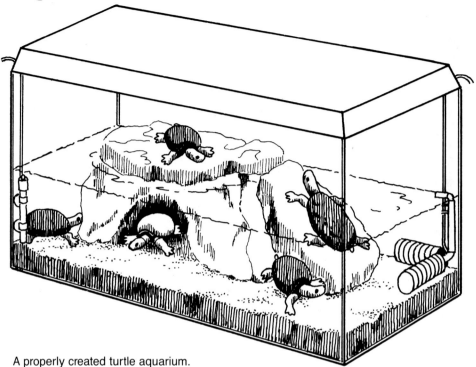

A properly created turtle aquarium.

The suitability of tap water for turtles can be improved with Tetra Contra-Chlorine Plus. Chlorine and chloramine can adversely affect your turtle's eyes. The new water being added should be of the same temperature as the old so as not to shock or chill your turtle.

Most semi-aquatic turtles are baskers. That is, in nature they clamber onto sloping shores, emergent debris, or even mats of surface vegetation, and sunbathe. This provides numerous benefits. It allows them to bring their body temperatures to optimum level, thus enhancing alertness, activity, and bodily functions. Prolonged basking also discourages ectoparasites such as leeches and other unwelcome "guests." When the surrounding waters are cool, turtles bask most persistently.

To be able to do so is important to their psychological well-being, even in captivity.

My specimens are allowed to bask beneath a full-spectrum (Vita-Lite® or similar) fluorescent bulb as well as provided with the heat and illumination from a strategically placed incandescent plant-growth bulb. Even here in southern Florida my turtles bask for long periods.

Other species of baby semi-aquatic turtles are occasionally available. Among these are River Sliders, genus *Pseudemys,* Soft-Shelled Turtles, genus *Trionyx,* and Common Snapping Turtles, genus *Chelydra.* Most make hardy and interesting captives, at least while young.

Please note: The substrate and basking areas provided for Soft-

Tetra ContraChlorine Plus.

Shelled Turtles MUST be entirely non-abrasive. Well water-logged or even algae-covered driftwood is ideal for Soft-Shells. Rough surfaces will cause plastral ulcers.

Strangely, some of our most aquatic species are relatively weak swimmers, hence not well adapted to life in a straight-sided aquarium. Among these are the several Mud Turtles, genus *Kinosternon,* Musk Turtles, genus *Sternotherus,* the grotesque-appearing Mata Mata Turtle, *Chelus fimbriatus,* and the Alligator Snapping Turtle, *Macroclemys temmincki.* All of these should be provided with water shallow enough for them to breathe easily while resting on the bottom with their necks fully extended. Although hauling-out areas illuminated by full-spectrum bulbs should be provided for them, few of these species bask regularly.

Common Musk Turtle, *Sternotherus odoratus*.

Red-Cheeked Mud Turtle, *Kinoster-non cruentatum*.

Box Turtles, genus *Terrapene,* Spotted, Wood, and Bog Turtles, genus *Clemmys,* and some Tortoises will be discussed in the chapters on semi-aquatic, woodland, and desert terraria.

For additional information I refer you to the Tetra Press publication entitled *Turtles, Terrapins, and Tortoises*.

Alligator Snapping Turtle, *Macroclemys temmincki,* hatching.

Semi-Aquatic Terrarium

Like the aquatic terrarium/aquarium, the semi-aquatic terrarium may be as simple or as complex as you wish. The more complex it is, the more difficult it will be to clean on the rare occasions when maintenance is necessary.

A semi-aquatic terrarium is just that . . . an environment that provides both a water and a land area for its inhabitants. It is imperative that the one be entirely separated from the other, lest the land area become soggy and sour and the water perpetually dirty. There are at least two ways that this separation can be accomplished:

1. Cut a suitably sized piece of glass and seal it firmly in place with latex aquarium sealant. It should be situated on a gentle slope, the top towards the land area. Both sides and the bottom MUST be tightly sealed. It is a good idea to run a thin bead of sealant along the top edge as well, to forestall the possibility of an inhabitant scraping itself on a sharp edge. To make the land area even more easily accessible, a film of sealant may be spread on the glass surface that slopes from the water and a covering of fine, smooth sand sprinkled on this before it dries. This will allow adequate toeholds for even the smallest of inhabitants. In this kind of set-up it is desirable to provide some type of filtration to assist in keeping the water clean.

2. The simple method, the one that I use extensively, is to provide the water in a rather shallow, easily removed receptacle. My favorites, depending on the amount of water wanted, are plastic shoe and sweater boxes. In these you can provide water to a depth of 2 to 2½ inches. Natural-appearing egress ramps may be made by the prudent use of cork bark. The advantages of this set-up are obvious. You merely lift the water pan out, thoroughly clean it, refill, and replace. Little muss, no fuss, and almost no bother.

The design and plantings of the land area can be handled in one of several ways. First, decide what type of substrate you will use. You have several choices. If you wish to maintain amphibians you may choose a substrate of dampened, unmilled sphagnum moss. This is also ideal for small semi-terrestrial turtles such as Bog Turtles. Another choice would be cypress bark mulch or fibers. This is ideal for larger turtles and small Caimans. Such substrates as these have the advantage of being resilient, inexpensive, and easily replaced when they do become saturated or dirty. Some persons may prefer that the land area simply be filled with sand. Do keep in mind, though, that sand or loam is easily carried into the water area by active reptiles and amphibians, necessitating frequent cleaning. Decorative plants may be left in pots which are then sunk to their rims in the substrate.

More natural substrates, in which

Semi-Aquatic Terrarium: Style 1.

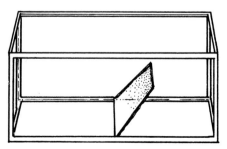

Semi-Aquatic Terrarium: Style 2.

mosses and small woodland plants grow directly, are somewhat more complex to maintain. But for those of you who revel in such intricacies I offer the following suggestions.

First place a one-inch layer of activated charcoal on the bottom of your tank. I like to keep this separated from the subsequent layers by spreading a sheet of air-conditioning filter material on top of the charcoal. On top of the filter place a layer of coarse gravel, then, on top of the gravel, a thick layer of potting soil or woodland humus. The plants will grow directly in this.

While either method can produce attractive results, the first offers definite ease of maintenance. The second is considerably more intricate.

The kinds of plants to be used will, like the substrate, depend on what kind of animal specimens the terrarium is to house. While maidenhair ferns and other delicate plant species would thrive in a set-up housing tiny Arrow-Poison or Tree Frogs, such plants would soon be laid flat by a boisterous 15-inch Caiman. For this latter animal, more robust specimen plants, perhaps sturdy-stemmed dracaenas, or "Chinese evergreens," would be in order. Suitable aquatic plants may also be utilized as desired.

Besides plants, attractively shaped pieces of driftwood, moss-covered logs, or appropriate rock formations may be used for decoration in both land and water areas.

The following species are suitable for semi-aquatic terraria.

Two ideal terrarium plants: (above) fittonia and (below) prayer plant.

Tiger and Spotted Salamanders, and related Ambystomatid species

Other name: Mole Salamanders
Ambystoma tigrinum ssp., *A. maculatum,* and others

Size: Tiger Salamanders regularly exceed a robust 8 inches. Spotted and other commonly offered related salamanders are of a considerably lesser bulk.

Description: The members of this group are, when adult, persistent woodland burrowers. The larvae are aquatic and frequently sold as Axolotls or Water Dogs. Adults have large heads, small rather protuberant eyes, and short, but efficient, legs. While plainly colored as larvae and newly metamorphosed juveniles, a few species develop rather striking markings of contrasting colors when adult.

Barred Tiger Salamander, *Ambystoma tigrinum mavortium.*

According to subspecies, Tiger Salamanders may vary from obscurely marked, muddy greenish, or grayish animals to those with a well-defined barred or reticulated pattern of ocher or tan against a ground color of black.

Spotted Salamanders are appropriately named. Along each side of the dark brown to slate-gray dorsum there occurs a regular to irregular line of few to many, yellowish spots.

Other species may have attractive saddles or crossbars of silver or pale gray. If of robust conformation and 4½ inches or less in length, it is probably the Marbled Salamander, *A. opacum;* if slender and more than 5 inches in length, it is more likely the Ringed Salamander, *A. annulatum.* Many other species are drab and less attractive.

Preferred temperature: 65 to 75 degrees.

Food: Terrestrial adults of these species are less apt to accept prepared foods than the aquatic larvae. They usually require worms and suitable in-

sect larvae if they are to be kept successfully. Large specimens may be cannibalistic.

Care: Suggested substrate: Several inches of fresh soil, humus, or sphagnum moss, damp, NOT WET, in consistency.

In spite of the fact that certain of the Mole Salamanders come from latitudes as far south as central Florida, south Texas, and even Mexico, they are creatures that prefer cool temperatures. In Florida and Texas they are most active during the cool rains of winter evenings. In Mexico they often dwell in the coolness of mountain fastnesses. During periods of excessive heat they burrow deeply and aestivate. Hence, as captives, they are happiest when in a cool climate or when their terrarium is kept in an air-conditioned room.

Japanese Fire-Bellied Newt
Cynops pyrrhogaster

Size: To 5 inches.

Description: A beautiful species, this pet store staple is a rich russet to dark brown dorsally. Its common name is derived from the color of its venter: red to red-orange vermiculated with dark. The skin of this species is glandular, and well-developed parotoid (nape) glands are present. While distinct from the neck, the head is well-proportioned and not especially angular.

At least two other Red-Bellied Newt species are occasionally offered as "Fire-Bellies." The first of these, also of Asiatic origin, is scientifically designated as *Paramesotriton hongkongiensis.* It is larger and more angular than the Japanese species. The second, an increasingly uncommon denizen of the Pacific U.S.A., designated

31

as *Taricha rivularis,* has an unmarked red to salmon venter.

Preferred temperature: 65 to 75 degrees.

Food: Suitably sized worms and insects are eagerly accepted. Most specimens will learn to forage for various Tetra brand foods while in the water.

Care: Suggested substrate: Several inches of fresh soil, humus, or sphagnum moss, damp, NOT WET, in consistency. Terrestrial except when breeding, these salamanders are denizens of cool woodland habitats. With proper care all will thrive for decades in a semi-aquatic terrarium.

Please note: While a great many newt species are offered as aquarium animals, most are not biologically suited for a life of perpetual immersion. They need, and deserve, a semi-aquatic environment.

Emperor Newt
Other name: Mandarin Newt
Tylototriton verrucosum

Size: Regularly attains 6 inches.

Description: This is one of the most impressive newts. The skin is highly glandular. Dorsally the species is an interesting and complex combination of slate-gray and bright orange. The top of the head is mostly orange. There is a broad, orange vertebral stripe and a glandular orange spot over the distal end of each rib. The legs, tail, and venter are mostly orange. Where not orange, the color is slate-gray to charcoal.

All other information is as described for the Fire-Bellied Newt.

Emperor Newts, *Tylototriton verrucosum.*

Fire Salamander, *Salamandra salamandra* ssp.

Fire Salamander
Salamandra salamandra ssp.

Size: Occasionally exceeds 6 inches.
Description: Although a member of the same family as the newts, the Fire Salamander is much more like a "typical" salamander in appearance. While glandular, the skin is relatively smooth and moist. Parotoid (nape) glands are conspicuous. Most specimens have a ground coloration of black with variable amounts of yellow, in the form of spots or stripes, dorsolaterally. Some specimens from the Italian highlands may be predominantly or entirely yellow.

All other information is as described for the Fire-Bellied Newt.

True Frogs
Other names: Leopard Frog, Wood Frog, Asiatic Green-Striped Frog, Bull Frog, and others
Rana sp.

Size: Variable. Most species are adult at between 2 and 4 inches, some are smaller, and others nearly twice that length.
Description: These are the "typical" frogs, sharp-nosed, long-legged, and agile. Some may be adorned with dark masks, some with well-defined spots or stripes, and others may be devoid of contrasting markings. The ground color may vary from various shades of brown to equally variable greens, singly or in combination. Pink-eyed albinos of the Bull and Leopard Frogs have been developed.
Preferred temperature: Whether of tropical or temperate origin, most species seem comfortable at a temperature of 68 to 80 degrees.
Food: While most specimens are avid predators upon worms and arthropods, larger species are persistently can-

33

Asiatic Green-Striped Frog, *Rana erythraea.*

nibalistic and can engulf surprisingly large prey.

Care: Suggested substrate: Fresh soil, humus, or sphagnum moss—damp, NOT WET, in consistency, is satisfactory for small and medium-sized species. Less adherent or easily moved substrate such as cypress bark mulch may be more desirable for larger species.

In nature many true frog species are pond and streamside dwellers, hence well adapted for life in the semi-aquatic terrarium. They should not be overcrowded. It is imperative that their water remain clean and fresh.

Frogs from temperate areas are also ideal inhabitants of an outdoor Tetra Pond and Fernery. See the appropriate designation for suggestions.

Horned Frogs
Ceratophrys, Proceratophrys, and *Odontophrynus* sp.

Size: Variable by sex and species. While males of the Colombian Horned Frog, *C. calcarata,* are adult at about a 2-inch length, females of the Argentine Horned Frogs, *C. ornata,* may near dinner-plate size, both in length and breadth.

Description: These are squat, angular frogs of tropical American origin, with an immense head, powerful jaws, and cannibalistic habits. Colors, and patterns, again variable by species and to a lesser extent by sex, range from tan and russet through bright green. The common name is derived from the presence of a supraocular "horn," a fleshy appendage on the upper eyelid which is little more than a nubbin in the large Argentine Horned Frog, but quite prominent in the smaller Surinam species, *C. aurita.*

Preferred temperature: 74 to 85 degrees seems perfectly satisfactory for all Horned Frog species.

Food: With a large head and prodigious appetite, the range of items considered food by a Horned Frog is mind-boggling. Large species will unhesitatingly tackle (usually successfully) animals up to the size of adult mice or small rats, other frogs, live fish, and fingers. Smaller species are necessarily more limited in their food intake, but are willing and entirely capable of overcoming small mice and large beetles.

Care: Cleanliness, suitable temperature, and ample food supply are all that Horned Frogs require to attain ripe old captive ages. They are being bred extensively in captivity in both pure and hybrid form.

Please note: Captive Horned Frogs can be remarkably aggressive. Toothlike processes are present in their jaws. A bite by even a modestly sized spec-imen can be quite painful. Watch where you place your fingers!

Bog Turtle

Other name: Muhlenberg's Turtle
Clemmys muhlenbergi
Size: Commonly attains a shell length of 4 inches.
Description: This uncommon species is one of the prettiest and most alert of the semi-terrestrial turtles.

The carapace (upper shell) is a warm or olive brown with vague to conspicuous darker radiations. The laminae (scales) often bear prominent areolae (growth rings). The plastron (lower shell) is predominantly black but has yellow highlights. The head is brown with darker vermiculations. Brilliant orange cheek patches are usually

Surinam Horned Frog, *Ceratophrys aurita.*

Bog Turtle, *Clemmys muhlenbergi*.

large, conspicuous, and are diagnostic of the species. However, with age the orange cheeks may become increasingly suffused with dark pigment. The legs are brownish to terra-cotta.

Preferred temperature: This species seems most comfortable if temperatures are maintained between 68 and 76 degrees. It does enjoy a hot spot where it may bask.

Food: Worms, insects, pinkie mice, Tetra ReptoMin, and raw meat are accepted by this species. They are capable of feeding either in or out of the water.

Care: Suggested substrate: Several inches of unmilled sphagnum upon which are laid a few large, convex pieces of cork bark to provide areas of seclusion.

These alert, personable, and attractive little turtles thrive in a room-temperature terrarium. They actively construct runways and burrows in their substrate and may choose one as "home," retiring there to rest or sleep. If undisturbed they tend to travel beneath, rather than over, the stems of recumbent plants, hence cause little, if any, damage to the plantings. They will soon learn to accept food from your fingers and, although capable of eating the food in terrestrial situations, often prefer to carry it to their water receptacle. For this reason, and because the species is not persistently aquatic, I use an easily cleaned plastic shoe box for the water bowl.

Please note: The Bog Turtle is considered a threatened or endangered species by several of the states to which it is native. Please ascertain that your specimens are legally procured. Captive-bred babies are occasionally available.

Budgett's Frog, *Lepidobatrachus laevis*. This primarily aquatic ceratophrine species is unusual in appearance and seldom seen.

Spotted Turtle, *Clemmys guttata*.

Spotted Turtle
Clemmys guttata
Size: This species occasionally attains a 5-inch shell length but is usually smaller.
Description: The Spotted Turtle is essentially black dorsally, with small, rounded, yellow spots on head and carapace. The spots may be sparse to numerous or, rarely, almost entirely lacking. Some specimens tend to have yellow or orangish cheek patches. The limbs and plastron are highlighted with orange or yellow. Juveniles typically have fewer spots, often no more than one to each carapacial plate.
Preferred temperature: 70 to 76 degrees, with a hot spot for basking.
Food: Worms, insects, Tetra ReptoMin, fish, and some raw meat.
Care: This is a more aquatic species than the Bog Turtle, to which it is closely related. For this reason it should be offered a greater volume of water than the latter. The Spotted Turtle prefers to feed while submerged.

Wood Turtle, *Clemmys insculpta.*

While their small size renders them well suited to indoor terraria, they are also excellent candidates for outdoor Tetra Ponds or Ferneries.

Wood Turtle
Clemmys insculpta
Size: To 10-inch carapace length.
Description: The Wood Turtle is the largest member of the genus. It is easily identified by its rather plain brown carapace, yellow and black plastron, and the fact that neck, limbs, and tail are suffused with russet, orange, terra-cotta, or yellow-orange.
Preferred temperature: This is a species of the cool, wooded northeastern United States and southeastern Canada. As such, it prefers a somewhat cool environment (72 to 78 degrees) that is provided with a hot spot for basking.
Food: They accept Tetra-Terrafauna Land Turtle and Tortoise Food, as well as worms, insects, and prepared catfoods. Some specimens relish ripe fruits.

European Pond Turtle, *Emys orbicularis*.

Care: Because of the large size when adult, only juveniles would make suitable semi-aquatic terrarium inhabitants. Adults make ideal, long-lived inhabitants of the Tetra Pond or Fernery (see page 67). The species is basically terrestrial from late spring, through the summer, and into mid-autumn. For the remaining months Wood Turtles are nearly entirely aquatic, even hibernating while submerged.

brilliantly patterned and have immensely long tails.

Preferred temperature: 74 to 82 degrees.

Food: European Pond Turtles often forage terrestrially.

Care: Similar to that discussed for the Spotted Turtle.

European Pond Turtle
Emys orbicularis ssp.

Size: While some rare individuals near one foot in shell length, those of many populations seldom exceed 5 inches.

Description: This is another attractive, but dark, turtle. Dorsally the ground color is black or olive-black. Both on the carapace and the head there are myriad yellowish dash or teardrop markings. The plastron is yellowish with black highlights. Juveniles are more

Other Turtle Species

Juveniles of a great many other turtle species are ideally suited for the semi-aquatic terrarium. However, if properly cared for, most will soon outgrow the space allotted to them. If a long-term commitment is desired it will then be necessary to provide larger quarters. For most aquatic and semi-aquatic species Tetra Ponds are ideal.

Spectacled Caiman
Other name: South American Alligator

Caiman crocodylus ssp.

Size: Unfortunately, if well fed and kept in an adequately sized terrarium, the interesting little pet shop Caiman does not remain little for long. Adults may exceed 8 feet in overall length.

Description: This is an olive-colored, alligator-like crocodilian with a raised, bony bridge across the base of its rather broad snout. Anterior to the eyes, this forms the bridge of the spectacle from which the species derives its name. Black crossbands may be present on both body and tail.

Preferred temperature: 78 to 84 degrees is suitable for this tropical species. A hot spot for basking should be provided.

Food: Fish, mice, and meat are all grist for the mill of this usually ill-tempered crocodilian.

Care: If warm temperatures prevail and space is ample in its container, your Caiman should feed avidly and grow quickly. Growth may be stunted if either condition is sub-optimal. Often purchased on impulse, Caimans usually quickly prove more of a challenge than their owners can easily handle. You should carefully consider BEFORE your purchase exactly how you intend to provide for a bad-tempered, 6-foot-long crocodilian.

Although the sturdy legs of the Caiman are quite capable of raising the body well above the ground, Caimans often drag themselves to and from the water. A substrate of sizeable pebbles or cypress bark mulch will be less apt to be tracked into the water than humus or sand.

Spectacled Caiman, *Caiman crocodylus* ssp.

Basilisk Lizards
Genus *Basiliscus*

Mexican Basilisk, *Basiliscus vittatus* (adult male).

Size: Males are very much larger, and far more ornate, than females. Males frequently exceed 24 inches in length; females seldom more than 16 inches.

Description: The four species of Basilisks are among the most interesting of lizards. Unfortunately, they are slow to tame and frequently dash headlong into the glass of their terrarium at even the slightest disturbance. Permanent or recurring injuries to their noses are typical results.

Two Basilisk species, the Mexican, *B. vittatus,* and the Brown, *B. basiliscus* ssp., are cloaked in hues of tan, cream, and brown. Adult males of the Mexican Basilisk have well-developed head crests but poorly developed body and tail crests. These latter two ornamentations are much better developed on the Brown Basilisk, which also has a well-developed head crest. Color alone will distinguish the aptly named Green

Basilisk, *B. plumifrons.* Males have well-developed head, body, and tail crests. The fourth species, *B. galeritus,* has no common name. It is clad in russet and green and has only the head crest well developed. The vertebral and caudal crests are represented by enlarged, serrate scales.

Preferred temperature: 78 to 86 degrees. A warmed, arboreal perch should also be provided.

Food: Smaller specimens prefer vitamin-dusted crickets and other insects. Larger ones will eagerly accept suitably sized mice as well as insects.

Care: While among the most attractive of the lizards, their excessive nervousness does little to endear Basilisks to most keepers. Some do tame, however. Take care to move slowly when in the proximity of their terrarium. Some keepers cover all of the outside of the

41

Crocodile Lizard, *Shinisaurus croc-odylurus.*

terrarium except a small viewing area with paper or opaque aquarium paint. Reflective window tinting film is also said to be effective.

Not only do these lizards swim well, they move so fast that they are able to run across the surface film of quiet waters without breaking through. They also are quite adept at climbing and often bask on sunlit branches overhanging water bodies.

Provide ample space, security, and water for your Basilisks.

Crocodile Lizard
Shinisaurus crocodylurus

Size: Males, the larger sex, attain an adult length of 12 to 15 inches.

Description: This is an interesting little lizard that is being seen with increasing frequency. The head outline is convex in profile. Two dark-bordered light lines radiate downward from beneath the eye. The coarsely granular scales are heaviest dorsally. The muscular, later-ally flattened tail is a powerful organ of aquatic propulsion. The color, darkest dorsally, is gray, olive-gray, or even darker. Darker bands are usually visible. These are most visible laterally and on the tail.

Preferred temperature: 78 to 86 degrees. A warmed, arboreal basking spot should be provided.

Food: Goldfish, tadpoles, and other aquatic organisms, as well as crickets and grasshoppers, are acceptable food items.

Care: Suggested substrate: Cypress bark mulch or other easily maintained material. Sturdy branches should be provided for climbing and basking.

I find this little Chinese lizard to be among the most interesting of the possibilities for the semi-aquatic terrarium. It often basks on branches above the water from which it can drop or leap directly to the safety of that aquatic environment. The several young are born alive.

Dry-Land Terraria

As implied by the name, the water content of dry-land terraria is reduced to that contained in water dishes. Two styles, the woodland terrarium and the desert terrarium, are the most frequently seen.

As with the land area of the semi-aquatic terrarium, the construction and planting of these terraria can be as simple or as complicated as you choose. The more complicated it is, the more detailed the maintenance will be.

The Woodland Terrarium

The woodland terrarium is merely a semi-aquatic terrarium without a pool of water. It may be a densely planted, humid affair or relatively dry and largely plant-free.

I ask that you refer to the set-up instructions for the land area of the semi-aquatic terrarium for the two most common methods of construction.

As with the semi-aquatic terrarium, it is IMPERATIVE that the soil or substrate not be allowed to become soggy and sour.

Among the more easily grown plants are the various philodendrons, syngoniums, spathyphyllums, bromeliads, fittonias, and other readily obtained greenhouse varieties.

The following species are suitable for the woodland terrarium.

Woodland, Brook, Spring, Red, Mud, and other Lungless Salamanders
Genera *Plethodon, Eurycea, Gyrinophilus, Pseudotriton,* and others

Size: Variable according to species. Some, such as the Red-Backed and Two-Lined Salamanders, are adult at a slender 3 to 4 inches in length. Others, among them the various Spring, Red, and Mud Salamanders, are proportionately more robust and may attain 6 or 7 inches in length.

Description: Among these several genera are some of the prettiest of the salamanders. Certainly the Mud, Red, and Spring Salamanders are colorful enough to qualify as flamboyant. The various races of the first two vary from reddish-tan to vermillion in ground color, and sport an equally variable number of jet-black dots. The several

Woodland terrarium.

43

Black-Chinned Red Salamander,
Pseudotriton ruber schenki.

races of the Spring Salamander, easily identified by their squared-off nose, may range from salmon to an attractive purplish-brown and they are usually profusely speckled with black. Among the prettiest of the Brook Salamander group are two species which often have an orange ground color. These are the Long-Tailed and the Cave Salamanders. The former is prettily speckled with black. The latter usually bears more prominent black dots and a conspicuous herringbone pattern on the sides of its tail. Other species of Brook Salamanders may be precisely striped with two (the Two-Lined Salamander) or three (the Three-Lined Salamander) well-defined dark lines against a tan or yellowish ground color. Several of the Woodland Salamanders may have straight-edged (the various Red-Backed Salamanders) or irregularly edged (the Zig-Zag Salamanders) red or tan stripes dorsally, and grayish sides. Most of these have confusingly similar-appearing all-dark phases. I consider the prettiest of the Woodland Salamanders to be the large Yonahlossee. It has a dark head and tail surface, pearl-gray sides, and a terracotta back.

Preferred temperature: All of these interesting salamanders prefer their terraria somewhat on the cool side. Temperatures of from 65 to 72 degrees are ideal for most.

Food: Most terrestrial salamanders prefer live food. Tiny crickets, white worms, or suitably sized earthworms are ideal. Many will learn to accept pieces of raw meat presented to them on a gently manipulated broomstraw, but do keep in mind that this latter is not a balanced diet.

Care: None of these salamanders have lungs. All transpire through their thin, moist skins. They are unable to survive in dirty, dry, or stagnant quarters. The preferred substrates are a fresh, moist humus/loam mixture or moist sphagnum or other moss.

Arrow-Poison Frogs
Genera *Dendrobates, Phyllobates,* and others

Size: All species of the various genera are small. Many are adult at barely an inch in length, others near twice that size.

Description: So brilliantly colored are many of the Arrow-Poison Frog species that they have been likened to "animated jewels." The common names of some species are descriptive . . . Strawberry Frog, Green and Black Arrow-Poison Frog, Azure Arrow-Poison Frog, Fantastic Arrow-Poison Frog, and on, and on. Some, such as the Strawberry Frog, may have a rather unicolored body but rear limbs of a sharply contrasting midnight blue or black. The Azure Frog is just that, patterned with a variable amount of azure blue over a black ground color. One species, the Surinam Arrow-Poison Frog, is currently rather generally available, and has a black body with orange longitudinal stripes and midnight-blue legs with black mottlings.

Preferred temperature: These are all tropical frogs. They thrive at temperatures between 74 and 84 degrees.

Food: The small size of the various Arrow-Poison (also called Dart-Poison) Frogs makes a specialized diet mandatory. Newly hatched, vitamin-dusted crickets, wingless fruitflies, certain ants, aphids, and other small insects are all eagerly accepted. The crickets, which are available through your pet shop, may be used as the base diet.

Care: The collective group name, "Arrow-Poison Frogs," has been derived

Surinam Arrow-Poison Frog, *Dendrobates tinctorius*.

45

from the fact that certain of the species produce skin secretions of such toxicity that they are used by some Amerindian tribes to tip hunting arrows and darts. While the secretions produced by those species offered for sale in pet shops is of negligible virulency, it is sufficient to cause discomfort if brought in contact with mucous membranes. You should always wash your hands IMMEDIATELY after handling ANY amphibian. All, even indigenous forms, produce irritating protective secretions.

Arrow-Poison Frogs are best maintained monotypically—each species separated from the other—in family or breeding groups. Secure hiding places in the form of curved cork bark, halved coconut husks, and dense plantings should be provided. Enough of these should be present to allow each frog its own area of seclusion. Several members of this group prefer water in the

Cuban Tree Frog, *Osteopilus septentrionalis.*

cups and leaf axils of bromeliads for both dwelling and tadpole raising.

It is a good idea to have food insects present at all times.

Tree Frogs
Genera *Hyla, Agalychnis, Smilisca, Phrynohyas, Osteopilus, Litoria, Rhacophorus,* and others

Size: While most are of small to medium size (1 to 2½ inches), a few may near 5 inches in length.

Description: While somewhat diverse in both color and markings, most of the species offered as "tree frogs" are of some shade of brown, tan, gray, or green. Dorsal markings, if present, may take the shape of spots, ocelli, reticulations, or blotches. Of course, to be accepted by the pet trade as a Tree Frog, toe pads must be present.

Among the more commonly offered species are the Barking Tree Frog of

Red-Eyed Tree Frog, *Agalychnis callidryas.*

the southeastern United States and the immensely popular Dumpy Tree Frog of Australia.

The former attains a size of about 2½ inches and may vary in color and markings from moment to moment. It has a granular skin, is often green (but may be brown), and usually has dark spots or ocelli present on the dorsum. Occasionally these may temporarily be yellow, or even lacking.

The Dumpy Tree Frog may occasionally attain, or even exceed, 4 inches in length. Its smooth, rather shiny skin may vary in hue from brown through jade to bright green. Of Australian origin, this species prefers to be supplied with a small water dish in otherwise dry surroundings.

One of the more beautiful species often available is the tropical American Red-Eyed Tree Frog. Its dorsal color is usually bright green, its flanks yellow, barred with blue, and its eyes a startling

vermillion. It is adult at about a 2-inch length.

Currently, several of the Southeast Asian "Flying Frogs" are available in pet shops. The most spectacular of these have a bright green dorsum and yellowish fingers and toes that are fully webbed with blue or black skin. While capable of gliding for fair distances, these highly arboreal creatures do not fly.

Species of several frog families possess adhesive toe pads that enable them to climb agilely.

Preferred temperature: To know the temperature preferences of your Tree Frogs you must first know their species. So many are available that you may have to rely on your pet dealer for information as to identification and origin. Most thrive at temperatures be-

47

tween 70 and 78 degrees.
Food: Food items may vary according to the size of your Tree Frogs. While most prefer vitamin-dusted crickets and other insects, some, such as the Dumpy Tree Frog, will eagerly accept newly born, or even larger, mice. Experiment. BEWARE! If Tree Frogs of disparate sizes are housed together, cannibalism may occur.
Care: All, except the Dumpy Tree Frog, will thrive in a normally moist terrarium. Males may often be induced to sing by lightly misting their terrarium home. The Dumpy Tree Frog prefers a dry terrarium (a folded newspaper-bottom covering seems best for this species) and a small water dish in which it may choose to sit occasionally.

Flying Frog, *Rhacophorus* sp.

Day Geckos
Genus *Phelsuma*

Size: The members of this group vary from 3½ to about 7 inches in length.
Description: Most, if not all of the species currently in the pet trade, are of some shade of green, usually Kelly or emerald. Against this many have markings of brilliant orange and some may be highlighted in turquoise or robin's-egg blue. These arboreal beauties have well-developed toe pads but lack eyelids.
Preferred temperature: 76 to 84 degrees.
Food: Most wild Day Geckos augment their insect diet with pollen or other sweet plant derivatives. An artificial substitute is necessary for captives. To formulate this, add to a jar of strained mixed-fruit dessert baby food an eye-dropperful of Avitron or other liquid vitamin, ½ tablespoon each of bee pollen and liquid vitamin C, and 5 cc of 20-percent calcium gluconate. Mix, then add enough water so that the Geckos can lap it up easily. Dust crickets with a vitamin powder. Waxworms are also eagerly accepted.
Care: The beautiful colorations displayed by the various Day Geckos make them well worth the extra work necessitated by their specialized dietary requirements.

The importance of vitamins and minerals in their diet cannot be over-emphasized, for Day Geckos are very prone to a malady variously called "limber" or "rubber-jaw." This is a softening of the bones caused by decalcification.

Secondarily, it must also be emphasized that Day Geckos are creatures to look at, not hold. Their integuments are delicate and will tear with even the most careful handling. A suitably sized net is helpful in moving Day Geckos.

These highly arboreal creatures ap-

Day Gecko, *Phelsuma* sp.

preciate a tall, well-planted terrarium with branches upon which they may climb.

They prefer to lap water droplets from freshly sprinkled leaves.

Anoles
Other name: American Chameleons
Genus *Anolis*

Size: While most are adult at 4 to 9 inches in length, a few exceed 12 inches.

Description: These are all very "typical" lizards in appearance and demeanor . . . slender-bodied, long-tailed, angular-headed insectivores. Most have well-developed toe pads. Although best known to most people for their color-changing abilities, not all Anoles are capable of extensive variation. One that is, however, is the very common Green Anole, *A. carolinensis.* This pretty, arboreal acrobat may be bright green one moment and dark

brown a little later. Males have a yellow to pink dewlap. The slightly larger Hispaniolan Green Anole, *A. chlorocyanus* ssp., remains some shade of green. It has whorls of enlarged scales at regular intervals around its tail and both sexes have dark dewlaps. It, too, is arboreal. The Brown Anole, *A. sagrei* ssp., is aptly named. Of Bahamian and West Indian origin, it is always some shade of tan or brown. Males, darker and much larger than females, have a light-edged yellow or pink dewlap. The largest of the genus is the Knight Anole, *A. equestris* ssp. These 18-inch-long creatures are of Cuban origin (now an established alien species in Dade and Broward Counties in south Florida) and may be better cared for in a cage than a terrarium. They are extensively arboreal, quickly languishing if spacious quarters and tree limbs are not provided. While usually of a bright green color, they, at times, may take on a velvety blackish-brown hue. No matter the immediate color, a bold yellow mark is prominent along the lower jaw and another over the shoulder. Both sexes have immense red dewlaps.

Preferred temperature: Most of these lizards are tropical sun worshippers. A temperature of 74 to 84 degrees is fine but should be augmented with an arboreal hot spot for basking.

Food: Vitamin-dusted crickets, mealworms, waxworms, and other insects should be provided for the smaller species. The larger species may also accept the petals of blossoms and, occasionally, ripe fruit. Knight Anoles may also eat small mice.

Care: Adequate space, a well-rounded diet, suitable temperatures, and branches for climbing are the requisites for maintaining Anoles. They prefer to lap water droplets from leaves.

Five-Lined, Southeastern Five-Lined, and Broad-Headed Skinks
Eumeces fasciatus, E. inexpectatus, and E. laticeps

Size: The first two are adult at about 7 inches in length. The Broad-Headed Skink nears 12 inches.

Description: Juveniles of all three species differ greatly in appearance from the adults. All three are confusingly similar so a separation from one another will not be attempted here. Juveniles are black, patterned with five bright-yellow stripes dorsally. The tails are electric blue. Adults are much less gaudy. They have brown bodies (occasionally retaining remnants of the striping) and tails. However, sexually mature males develop fiery orange heads during the spring and early summer breeding season.

Preferred temperature: 70 to 80 degrees is ideal for most skinks. A hot

Knight Anole, *Anolis e. equestris.*

spot should be provided for basking.
Food: While in the wild most American skinks are largely insectivorous, captives may be induced to accept canned catfoods as well.
Care: These shiny, attractive lizards are common woodland denizens over much of the eastern U.S.A. They are often most common along watercourses or on floodplains. While all climb, the large Broad-Headed Skink is primarily arboreal. Although they do not require the high temperatures so necessary to desert lizards, they do enjoy a hot spot for basking.

Small Woodland Snakes

Other names: Ring-Necked, Brown, Red-Bellied, and Green Snakes, and others
Genera *Diadophis, Storeria,* and *Opheodrys*
Size: Except for the Rough Green

Broad-Headed Skink, *Eumeces laticeps.*

Snake, which can attain nearly a yard in length, these species are fully adult at less than an 18-inch length. Most specimens are much smaller.
Description: The several races of Ring-Necked Snake usually sport a slate-gray dorsum, a narrow orange collar (which may be entire or broken middorsally), and an orange venter (often brighter on the tail) that may, or may not, be marked with series of small, black halfmoons. The Brown and Red-Bellied Snakes are closely related to one another. Both have a brown (rarely gray or charcoal) dorsum, vestiges of a paler neck ring, and a pink or flesh-colored belly (Brown Snakes), or a red, red-orange, or rarely charcoal belly (Red-Bellied Snakes). The two species of Green Snakes are just that . . . green dorsally . . . except when newly born or ready to shed their skins.

Southern Ring-Necked Snake, *Diadophis p. punctatus*.

Then they are much duller, often slaty. The venters of both are yellow. The largely arboreal Rough Green Snake is the larger, often exceeding 24 inches in length, and has keeled dorsal scales. The Smooth Green Snake is a primarily terrestrial resident of open woodland undergrowth, meadow edges, and other such densely vegetated areas.

Preferred temperature: These secretive snakes are usually found in or near cool woodlands. A temperature of 72 to 78 is ideal. A hot spot should be provided for basking, even if seldom used.

Food: All feed on insects, worms, and spiders. Experiment. The Rough Green Snake is especially fond of smooth caterpillars and crickets.

Care: Although these are all ideal specimens for the woodland terrarium, they will develop skin lesions if the substrate becomes too damp. Take care not to overwater. Provide branches or tall plants for the Rough Green Snake to climb in.

The Desert Terrarium

The desert terrarium is intended to house semi-arid and arid land species of reptiles and amphibians. The intent is to provide a home as dry as that in which the inhabitants have evolved. With that in mind, it is best if a substrate of fine sand (washed builder's sand is excellent) is utilized, and that the plantings be both sparse and of drought-tolerant kinds. The simple mistake of using plants that require frequent watering may keep the humidity at a level

unsuitably high for the long-term well-being of the animal inhabitants. To further restrict the dispersal of the water through capillary action of the sand, I strongly recommend that the plants be retained in their own individual pots. As would be expected, cacti and succulents, with their varied appearances, make fine plant candidates. Full-spectrum lighting is a must to assure the health of both plant and animal inhabitants. It is by the reptile inhabitants of this terrarium type that appropriately sized Tetra-Terrafauna Sizzle Stones® or Hot Blocks® are most fully appreciated. Most desert reptiles (especially lizards and tortoises) quickly learn to use these important basking areas, especially when the latter are well illuminated. It is important that you follow the instructions provided with your Sizzle Stones and Hot Blocks. Failure to do so may cause injury to your animal inhabitants. Desert reptiles are used to rapid, and dramatic, temperature drops at night.
Please note: Horned Lizards, often the first-thought-of candidates for the desert terrarium, DO NOT make suitable captives. These specialized insectivores feed primarily on ants, a diet nearly impossible to duplicate in captivity.

While many snakes and tortoises are desert dwellers, they are best maintained on a paper, shaving, or carpet substrate. The latter is best for tortoises. Sand can be accidentally ingested and may cause fatal intestinal blockages.

The following species are suitable for the desert terrarium.

Banded, Leopard, and Fat-Tailed Geckos
Genera *Coleonyx, Eublepharus,* and *Hemitheconyx*

Size: The Banded Geckos of the United States are rather small, being adult at about 4 inches. The Leopard Gecko—a species from Pakistan and surrounding countries—and the West African Fat-Tailed Gecko are about twice that size when fully grown.
Description: Eublepharine geckos are nocturnal, have eyelids, and lack toe pads. They have yellowish or tan (Banded and Leopard Geckos) or brownish or gray (Fat-Tailed Geckos) ground colors. Darker bands are usually evident. These are the most prominent on young individuals, and with increasing age they may disintegrate into spots or flecks. The Fat-Tailed Gecko

Desert terrarium.

tends to have broader bands and to retain them throughout its life. Some individuals of this latter species have a narrow white middorsal line.

Preferred temperature: These creatures of the darkness emerge from their lairs after the intense daytime heat of the deserts and savannahs has dissipated somewhat. They are comfortable at 72 to 80 degrees. Many will use a warmed basking area if it is provided.

Food: Vitamin-dusted crickets and waxworms are quite adequate as a base diet for these lizards. The large Leopard and Fat-Tailed Geckos will usually enjoy rounding their diets off with newly born mice.

Care: As with other nocturnal creatures, full-spectrum lighting is not necessary to the well-being of these geckos. Care should be used when handling them, for their tails are easily autotomized (broken off). These crea-

Leopard Gecko, *Eublepharus macularius*.

tures thrive when well cared for. Life spans of ten to twenty years are not uncommon.

Collared Lizards
Genus *Crotaphytus*

Size: To nearly 12 inches, most of which is tail.

Description: Females are often of a very different color than the males. These are big-headed, thin-necked lizards with a rather squat, heavy body. Females are often of some shade of brown, tan, or gray (orange or red markings are present on sexually receptive individuals), and males are often a richer brown to green. Both sexes of most species have darker or lighter reticulations, spots, or bars. The head color of the males is often noticeably different from that of the body. The black collars from which the name is derived are best developed on

Collared Lizard, *Crotaphytus collaris* ssp.

the males.

Preferred temperature: These desert lizards are activated by the daytime warmth. A temperature of 76 to 84 degrees is adequate, but a hot spot for basking must be provided. Full-spectrum lighting should be used.

Food: While insects and an occasional blossom are the basic diet of this interesting species, Collared Lizards also eat smaller lizards, newly born mice, and freshly hatched birds.

Care: Providing the temperature is warm enough, the humidity low enough, and full-spectrum lighting is utilized, Collared Lizards will thrive. As with other desert lizards, temperatures can be allowed to drop by 10 or even 20 degrees at night. Collared Lizards have strong jaws and can pinch uncomfortably. When frightened they often open their mouths, displaying the dark interiors.

Chuckawallas and Desert Iguanas
Sauromalus sp. and *Dipsosaurus dorsalis* ssp.

Size: Both the Chuckawallas and Desert Iguanas are heavy-bodied lizards. The most commonly offered "Chucks" are adult at from 10 to 12 inches. Females are the smaller sex. Because of their comparatively longer tail, Desert Iguanas frequently exceed 12 inches.

Description: While quite dissimilar in appearance, both the Chuckawalla and the Desert Iguana are members of the same family. The former are rather dingy lizards, being of some shade of gray, brown, or reddish-brown. They have a blunt, rather abruptly terminated (not smoothly tapering) tail. When calm, Chuckawallas have rough, rather baggy, folded skin. When frightened in

Chuckawalla, *Sauromalus obesus* ssp.

the wild they clamber into rock crevices and inflate their bodies with air. The roughened skin pushing against the rock surfaces makes them nearly impossible to dislodge.

The well-proportioned Desert Iguana is of a gray or tan ground coloration with darker and lighter spots and reticulations.

Preferred temperature: These are creatures of the hot deserts. While an ambient temperature of from 80 to 86 degrees is satisfactory, they MUST have a hot spot that nears 100 degrees for basking, full-spectrum lighting, and very low relative humidity.

Food: Both species are omnivorous, accepting vitamin-dusted crickets, wax and mealworms, flower blossoms (dandelions seem a particular favorite), and some ripe fruit.

Care: Low relative humidity, a well-illuminated hot spot, and full-spectrum lighting are all necessities for successfully maintaining these interesting desert dwellers. If you are unable to provide these, you should avoid both species.

Tokay, *Gekko gecko.*

Desert Iguana, *Dipsosaurus d. dorsalis.*

57

Fence Lizards, Swifts, and Spiny Lizards
Genus *Sceloporus*

Size: This is a large genus with a multitude of species which range from just a few inches to more than a foot in length.
Description: All three of the common names are deserved. These are quick-moving lizards, with spiny, prominently keeled scales. They enjoy basking on elevated horizontal perches, including fence rails and fallen trees.

While most of these lizards have a ground color of some shade of gray with dark chevrons or bands, a few are clad in hues of blue, or even emerald green. The males of many species have prominent blue patches on the sides of the belly and throat. A few species may lack these entirely or have them of a rose or tan color.
Preferred temperature: Many of these lizards range well northward, others dwell in the comparative coolness of mountaintop fastnesses, and yet others dwell in the hot desert lowlands. ALL bask extensively. While from 76 to 82 degrees is satisfactory for an ambient temperature, hot spots for basking and full-spectrum lighting should be provided.
Food: Most are insectivorous, readily accepting vitamin-dusted crickets, waxworms, and mealworms. Some, especially the larger species, may occasionally sample blossoms.
Care: A great many members of this extensive genus are very easily kept. Among these are those species indigenous to the eastern U.S.A., as well as such desert dwellers as the Crevice Spiny, Desert Spiny, and Blue Spiny Lizards.

I have found the mountain-dwelling, tropical American, Emerald Swift to be difficult to maintain.

Provide all with a hot spot, full-spectrum lighting, and adequate vitamins.

Spiny Lizard, *Sceloporus* sp.

Alligator Lizards
Genera *Gerrhonotus, Elgaria,* and *Abronia*

Southern Alligator Lizard, *Gerrhonotus multicarinatus* ssp.

Size: While most specimens seen are less than 12 inches in length, some, especially tropical representatives, exceed this by a considerable amount.

Description: These are attenuated lizards with weak legs. They often move with a sinuous side-to-side motion, the legs tightly folded against their bodies. Along each side, from neck to groin, a lateral fold of skin may be seen. Their closest relatives are the legless Glass Lizards and Slow Worm Lizards. Certain species of the tropical but mountain-loving genus *Abronia* are extensively arboreal.

The several species of Alligator Lizards are of tan to gray (*Gerrhonotus* and *Elgaria*) or olive to rather bright green (*Abronia*) ground color. Most specimens are more brightly colored middorsally. Many, but not all, have darker crossbands or dorsal flecking.

Preferred temperature: A terrarium temperature of 68 to 78 degrees will suffice for these lizards as long as a hot spot for basking is provided.

Food: While insects are the primary part of the diet, Alligator Lizards also eat smaller lizards, tiny snakes, and newly born mice.

Care: These, for the most part, are among the most easily cared for of lizards. Although they thrive in the desert terrarium they will appreciate a water dish sufficiently large for them to crawl into entirely and soak. Keeping similarly sized specimens together will prevent cannibalism.

Homes for Herptiles

While seldom as pleasing aesthetically as the various terraria, cages are usually more suitable for the housing of most larger snakes, lizards, and tortoises.

A cage can be as big or as small as you and its inhabitants deem necessary, or desirable. Likewise its shape can vary. It may be proportionately low, providing maximum floorspace for terrestrial species, or proportionately tall for those with arboreal tendencies.

Equally diverse are the materials from which cages can be constructed. While being escape-proof is the first consideration, three others are nearly as important. These are that the cage's surfaces be impervious to moisture, that it be both adequately ventilated and illuminated, and that it be designed so that it may be cleaned easily.

Aquaria easily double as terraria. They are easily modified so that they fill all of the above requirements. Heavily framed, readily secured screen or wire tops are available for most sizes.

If you prefer to test your carpentry skills, glass-fronted, well-ventilated wooden structures can be made to fit into virtually any nook or cranny of your room. The outsides may be beautified with stains, paints, or Formica sheeting. The wooden inside surfaces may be stained and then sealed with any of the moisture-proof urethane coatings.

You might wish to vary the illumination according to the species being maintained. Although less is known about the true lighting requirements of snakes and nocturnal lizards than those of diurnal lizards and tortoises, it is a fact that snakes and nocturnal lizards will survive, even thrive and breed, for decades without full-spectrum lighting. However, when such lighting is provided, many species will bask beneath it, a habit which suggests that it is appreciated if not actually necessary. Heated areas can be provided for animals of all three groups, snakes, lizards, and tortoises, through the prudent and careful use of either Sizzle Stones or Hot Blocks. Additionally, for long-term success with diurnal lizards

A properly appointed cage.

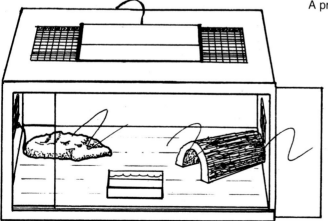

Green Iguana, *Iguana iguana* ssp.

and tortoises, full-spectrum lighting MUST be provided.

Water receptacles and "cage furniture" are two more considerations. Many reptiles enjoy having a water bowl of a size sufficient to allow them to immerse their entire body. This, of course, is especially true of those snake species which are semi-aquatic by nature. Other species utilize their water only for its primary purpose: drinking.

It is important that you keep in mind the fact that even those snakes and lizards that are semi-aquatic by nature need a thoroughly dry basking area when captive. In the wild the interim between dips is spent basking in the purifying rays of that broadest spectrum of lights, the sun. The sun quickly dries the animal and kills the bacteria that so rapidly promote skin problems in an artificial environment.

The use of cage furniture may, or may not, be a critical consideration.

Many of the less secretive reptile species will thrive in even a bare cage. However, both from the point of aesthetics and to give more retiring species a greater feeling of security, most hobbyists prefer to use cage furniture of some type. For some of the shyest captive reptiles, the ability to feel securely hidden from view may be an absolute necessity.

Tetra-Terrafauna Critter Logs® and Critter Stumps® (cleaned and bleached opuntia cactus skeletons) are among the finest materials available. Hollow-centered, with a latticework of small openings on all sides, and available in several lengths and diameters, this natural, lightweight material offers safe, secure perches and niches for many reptiles. Alternatives are innumerable, but few are as aesthetically pleasing. Among alternatives are gnarled branches, attractive

Carpet Python, *Python spilotes* ssp.
(Queensland phase).

stumps, and even parrakeet nesting boxes. Many reptile species will feel most secure if these are anchored midway in height or even at the top of a cage rather than on the floor. Arboreal species should be provided with a network of material at varying levels over and along which they may crawl.

The floor covering of your cage can be of any of several materials. While several thicknesses of newspapers quite likely will suffice, Tetra-Terrafauna pre-cut terrarium linings, Astro Turf, or vacuumed wood shavings will be more aesthetically pleasing. Should you choose the latter, either pine or aspen seems the best.

Two types of cage lighting should be considered. Each serves its own purpose. A fluorescent lighting fixture fitted with a full-spectrum bulb (such as Vita Lite or Ultra D) should be used for general illumination. Prudent use of an incandescent floodlight or spotlight (I prefer one of those used to induce plant growth) can provide both illumination and a warmed basking area. The incandescent bulbs can be used either separately or in conjunction with Sizzle Stones or Hot Blocks.

Some Reptile Species for Which Cages Are Suitable

Snakes: All snakes are carnivorous. In contrast to the popular belief that live food is a necessity, many snakes will readily accept freshly killed or even thawed frozen food items. However, certain individuals may insist on living prey. Some species (most Rat, Pine, and Bull Snakes, Boas and Pythons) will insist on endothermic food items such as mice, rats, hamsters, or chicks. For others (Garter, Ribbon,

Water, and the two species of Eastern Hog-Nosed Snakes, for example) ectothermic prey items such as toads, frogs, fish, or lizards are mandatory. Some snake species (Racers, Whip Snakes, Western Hog-Nosed, and King Snakes) will accept either ectothermic or endothermic prey items.

Cannibalism is well documented among Milk and King Snakes, and some other snake species. Care and vigilance are always of keynote importance.

Partially arboreal to entirely arboreal snake species:

Boa Constrictors, *Boa constrictor* ssp.

Tree Boas, genus *Corallus*

Green Tree Python, *Chondropython viridis*

Burmese, Reticulated, and Carpet Pythons, genus *Python*

Rat and Corn Snakes, genera *Elaphe, Gonyosoma,* and *Spalerosophis*

Primarily terrestrial snake species:

Racers and Whip Snakes, genera *Coluber* and *Masticophis*

Pine and Bull Snakes, genus *Pituophis*

Milk and King Snakes, genus *Lampropeltis*

Garter and Ribbon Snakes, genus *Thamnophis*

Water Snakes, genera *Nerodia* and *Natrix*

Lizards: A great many lizard species are now available in the pet trade. Among them are many which thrive in captivity, as well as a few which languish under all but the most specialized conditions. Additional types are mentioned in the sections on semiaquatic and dry-land terraria.

Many lizards, such as Monitors and Tegus, are carnivorous—accepting small mammals, birds, other rep-

Honduran Milk Snake, *Lampropeltis triangulum hondurensis*.

tiles, amphibians, insects, and eggs. Others, such as the various Blue-Tongued (and related) Skinks and Iguanas, are omnivorous. These consume not only birds, small mammals, amphibians, insects, and eggs, but certain leaves and blossoms as well. A few species are largely herbivorous. Among these are the various Old World Spiny-Tailed Lizards (genus *Uromastyx*), as well as our own Desert Iguana, *Dipsosaurus dorsalis*, and Chuckawallas, *Sauromalus* sp. However, most lizards are insectivorous. Even in this category there are specialists. Some, such as the several Horned Lizards, *Phrynosoma* sp., Flying Dragons, *Draco* sp., and the little Spiny-Tailed Tree Runners, *Uracentron* sp., feed primarily upon ants, hence are unsatisfactory captives. But most lizard species will thrive upon vitamin-dusted crickets, grasshoppers, and meal-

Blotched Blue-Tongued Skink, *Tiliqua nigrolutea*.

worms.

The few examples listed here are diurnal and bask to a greater or lesser degree.

Monitor Lizards and Tegus, genera *Varanus* and *Tupinambis,* are tropical carnivores. Several of the Monitors are semi-aquatic. As captives, some will accept canned catfood or a catfood/raw-egg mixture.

Blue-Tongued Skinks, *Tiliqua* sp., are of Australian and Indonesian origin. They are among the largest members of their family. All are hardy, accepting canned catfoods, small mice, insects, and fruit.

Iguanas (Common or Green, Spiny-Tailed, and Club-Tailed), genera *Iguana, Ctenosaura,* and *Enyliosaurus,* are of New World origin. In spite of being among the most common of the pet-shop lizards, these creatures are not the most easily kept as captives. Both the Common and Spiny-Tailed Iguanas commonly exceed 30 inches

Elongated Tortoise, *Geochelone elongata*.

in length when adult. It is not unusual for the former species to double that length. The Club-Tailed Iguanas are considerably smaller, seldom exceeding a foot in length. All MUST have full-spectrum lighting, a hot spot for basking, and vitamin/mineral supplements in a varied diet. Lettuce and/or blossoms, while both good supplements, do not, in themselves, constitute a satisfactory diet. Supply them with finely chopped or grated apples, bananas, avocados, mangos, papayas, squash, and other fruit and vegetables. Also provide crickets, some mealworms, and mice which vary in size from newly born to adult, according to the size of your lizard.

The diminutive Club-Tailed Iguanas are more apt to be principally insectivorous. However, most will accept newly born mice as a supplement. Offer them fruit and vegetables as well.

Tortoises and terrestrial turtles: There are only five truly terrestrial turtle and tortoise species native to the U.S.A. These are the Eastern Box Turtle, *Terrapene carolina* (four subspecies), and the Western Box Turtle, *Terrapene ornata* (two subspecies), and the three tortoises, the Gopher, the Texas, and the Desert, *Gopherus* sp. Not only are the tortoises notoriously difficult to keep if removed from their very specific habitats, but all are protected by state laws. Most states protect Box Turtles as well. None, except the four races of the Eastern Box Turtle, are tolerant of high humidity levels. This includes the Eastern Gopher Tortoise, which regulates its microenvironment by choosing a very specific ecological niche and then burrowing to further control temperature and humidity factors. A good rule of thumb is, if you dwell in areas of high humidity, restrict the species you keep to those originating in areas with such conditions. It is far easier to raise than to lower the relative humidity.

Turtles and tortoises are too well known to require general detail. They are among the few reptiles easily tolerated by most persons. Many of the true tortoises are largely, but few are exclusively, vegetarians. As captives, if humidity, temperature, and lighting requirements are met, most will thrive. A varied diet is best. This can consist of a base of Tetra-Terrafauna Land Turtle and Tortoise Food augmented by leafy vegetables such as romaine lettuce, escarole, and turnip greens, chopped or grated yellow vegetables, and a wide variety of fruit. In addition, the various Eastern Box Turtles, as well as most of the imported Asiatic and tropical American species, enjoy worms, and the Ornate and Desert Box Turtles are active, even agile, predators on grasshoppers and crickets.

I have found indoor/outdoor carpeting the best floor covering for turtles and tortoises. Paper coverings allow their feet to slip. This can cause deformities, especially in young, rapidly growing specimens. The deep pile of Astro Turf may be equally difficult for them to negotiate.

Species which thrive in high-humidity situations: Red-Footed Tortoise, Yellow-Footed Tortoises, and Elongated Tortoise, all of the genus *Geochelone* (terrestrial); Forest Hinge-Backed Tortoise, *Kinixys erosa* (terrestrial); Eastern Box Turtle, Gulf Coast Box Turtle, Florida Box Turtle, and Three-Toed Box Turtle, *Terrapene carolina* ssp. (terrestrial); Chinese Golden-Headed Box Turtle, *Cuora trifasciata* (semi-aquatic); Malayan Box Turtle, *Cuora amboinensis* (principally aquatic); Vietnamese Box Turtle, *Cuora galbinifrons* (principally terrestrial); Chinese Yellow-Margined Box Turtle, *Cuora flavomarginata* (principally terrestrial); Central American Wood Turtles, *Rhinoclemmys pulcherrima* ssp. (semi-aquatic).

Terrestrial species adapted to low-humidity situations: Leopard Tortoise, Spur-Thighed Tortoise, and Star Tortoise, all of the genus *Geochelone;* Savannah Hinge-Backed Tortoise, *Kinixys belliana;* Desert Box Turtle and Ornate Box Turtle, *Terrapene ornata* ssp.

Tetra Ponds or Ferneries

A natural extension of one's terrarium-keeping is a backyard or foyer pond. It is there, under even more natural settings, and with far more room than you can provide in a terrarium, that your fast-growing turtles or aquatic creatures can spend at least the warm months. The length of time that they can actually spend outdoors will be dictated by two factors: pond water temperature and the species involved.

In a garden pond in New England that did not freeze all the way to the bottom I had numerous year-round residents . . . Reeve's Turtles (of Japanese, not Southeast Asian, origin), European Pond Turtles, Painted Turtles, Red-Eared Sliders, and others. Besides these, I had an amazingly varied "walk-in trade." Green and Pickerel Frogs, American and Fowler's Toads, and even a Water Snake or two sur-mounted the low walls we had in place to restrain the wanderings of our turtles and took up seasonal residency.

Our next pond was constructed in central Florida. There, the more benign temperatures allowed a dramatic increase of the turtle species we kept. Again, in spite of the fact that we lived right in the city, four species of frogs moved in almost overnight. Within days Southern Toads, Eastern Narrow-Mouthed Toads, and Squirrel Tree Frogs called from the ferny banks, while a half dozen Green Tree Frogs made themselves at home among the emergent (but potted) cattails and water lilies.

Once, the enthusiasm to have a

A Tetra garden pond can be readily adapted to provide an extension of an indoor aquatic or semi-aquatic terrarium.

backyard pool might have been dimmed by the thought of the endless mixing and laying of cement, but this is no longer necessary. Tetra Ponds are a viable, easily-worked-with, long-lasting alternative. Tetra Pond Liners come in many sizes, the smallest making a whiskey-barrel pond, and the largest providing an ocean of water which measures 19 x 26 feet with a maximum depth of two feet. Even better, Tetra Ponds can be of "in-ground" (my preference) or, with the purchase of a few retaining timbers, "above-ground" design. Tetra's in-ground, 45-mil and 60-mil pond liners are so easy to install that they require only six steps, each carefully outlined on an instruction sheet.

The Tetra ClearChoice Biofilters and Tetra AquaZyme will aid you in maintaining sparkling, biologically safe water.

The beauty of a greenhouse or atrium can be enhanced by the presence of a Tetra Pond. There, protected from adverse weather conditions, beautified by creative lighting, a garden pond of unparalleled

Tetra Pond Liners

beauty can be constructed. In this way you can bring a little bit of the tropics to a home even in the northern-tier states. And you can diversify your interests dramatically in such a closed environment. Amidst the airy branches of such pond-edge greenhouse plantings as ficus and bottlebrush trees, you may wish to loose a pair or two of small, melodious finches. (Green or gray singing finches are perfect additions.) There they will often breed and perpetuate a balmy ambience within which you may at least temporarily escape the hustle and bustle of an all-too-busy world.

Tetra-Terrafauna Diet Supplements, Health Aids, and Other Selected Products

Many reptiles and amphibians will survive better if provided with regular diet supplements of vitamins and minerals. On occasion one from even the most fastidiously maintained collection may sicken or become so stressed that it requires some form of medication. I list here some of the Tetra-Terrafauna diet supplements, health aids, and cage accessories available in most pet shops. Read and carefully follow directions.

Diet Supplements

Reptovit® is a glucose-based, basic vitamin supplement. It will serve as an immediate, short-term stimulant for both lethargic reptiles and reluctant feeders. It is particularly useful when used with a newly acquired reptile that may not appear in the best of health.

Vitalife® is a more complex formula of vitamins and minerals designed to provide long-term benefits. It also contains gastric acids which aid in food digestion, and its fine consistency makes it easy to apply to live insects. Vitalife is also ideal for amphibians. It should be provided for established terrarium animals on a regular basis.

Reptocal should be used for larger, fast-growing reptiles such as large snakes, iguanas, and Monitor Lizards. Reptical is a calcium- and phosphorus-based mineral supplement which promotes healthy skeletal growth and prevents osteoporosis. Often referred to as the "sunshine substitute," it will also promote healthy growth and prevent shell softening in larger turtles.

Reptosol should be used through infancy to ensure that all reptiles and amphibians receive proper vitamin nutrition as they make the transition to an adult diet. It can be administered directly using the package dropper or

Diet supplements for reptiles and amphibians.

added to the drinking water.

Stimulap®, a liquid vitamin B-12 concentrate, is formulated to stimulate the appetite of the occasional reptile that is not feeding well.

Health Aids and Turtle/ Tortoise Foods

Turtles and tortoises are among the most frequently kept reptiles. Unfortunately, many keepers do not initially understand the complex needs of their shelled pets. If kept indoors, turtles and tortoises MUST be provided with full-spectrum lighting (Day Cycle and Night Cycle); dry, non-abrasive, hot spots for basking; (if aquatic) well-filtered, clean water for which Tetra foam filters are ideal helpmates (see photo, page 8); and a well-rounded, vitamin-mineral-enriched diet. Lacking

one or more of these necessities often results in shell and/or eye problems for your captive turtles.

The natural diet of aquatic turtles is very different from that of terrestrial species. For both, Tetra Terrafauna has specifically formulated foods—the Tetra Terrafauna Land Turtle and Tortoise Food and Tetra ReptoMin® which is the staple diet of most amphibians and aquatic reptiles, especially turtles. Vita Shell helps keep shell and body in top condition.

Besides supplements and foods, Tetra Terrafauna offers four health aids that are specifically designed to help stressed turtles. Turtle Sulfa Bath® combats fungal infections of both shell and skin. Rid Rot® kills not only fungi, but many gram-negative and gram-positive bacteria, yeasts, viruses, and protozoa as well. Used together, as directed, they will assist in the treatment

Tetra ReptoMin is the staple diet of most amphibians and aquatic reptiles.

Health aids and treatments for turtles.

of many problems that may arise.

Turtle Eye Rinse and Turtle Eye Clear should be used as directed to help open and clear puffy, encrusted, or closed eyes.

Besides being used to treat ailing turtles, Rid Rot is an effective agent for combating mouth rot (infectious stomatitis), burns, and lesions present on other reptiles.

One of the most persistent problems faced by the collector of reptiles is the presence of internal parasites. These are particularly prevalent in wild-caught specimens. Among the most commonly encountered are the various roundworms, tapeworms, and flukes. Tetra-Terrafauna's Rid Worm® safely and effectively destroys many of these omnipresent pests.

Mites and ticks are among the most commonly encountered ectoparasites. Rid Mite® effectively kills, and prevents the recurrence of, most reptilian ectoparasites.

Occasionally a snake or lizard has problems shedding its skin. This usually occurs only if caging conditions are adverse, the humidity is too low, or the specimen is unhealthy. Most specimens will voluntarily soak in water receptacles or amidst dampened sphagnum or Evergreen Moss in preparation for their periodic sheds. It is imperative for the health of your specimen that it shed all of its skin at the proper time. With snakes, shedding occurs several days after the eyes, clouded in the initial stages, have cleared. It may be more difficult to determine the proper timing with lizards. Most lizards shed their skins in patches, while the shed skin of most healthy snakes is entire. The simple expedient of raising humidity or providing a soaking bowl will usually permit your reptiles to shed normally. Rarely, they may need additional help. Shed Aid®, a wetting solution, may be added to the water of the soaking container in these cases.

Reed's Iguana and Tortoise Foods

When it comes to nourishing reptiles the natural way, Reed's Iguana and Tortoise foods are the best choice for a complete and balanced diet. The Juvenile formula is ideal for young iguanas up to three years old. Older iguanas need the Adult formula to support their maturing dietary requirements. Both of Reed's formulas provide full-spectrum color enhancers to bring out the beautiful natural color in your iguana but do not contain animal by-products and is not high in protein. In addition, potentially toxic vitamin A is replaced with beta-carotene. Reed's food from Tetra is the best primary diet choice to assure the growth and health of your iguana.

A green iguana raised on Reed's Food.

Reed's Food from Tetra.

72

Viquarium Kits

The Water's Edge Viquarium offers a truly unique opportunity. It can convert an ordinary aquarium into a combination of an aquarium and a terrarium. Create a slice of nature where fish, amphibians and reptiles all live together. Also available is the Cascading Creek Viquarium, which features a lifelike waterfall and recessed gravel/planter areas.

There are a variety of accessories available to enhance your habitat. Tetra offers lifelike Plantastic Plants to beautify the aquarium portion of the tank. Terrarium Moss creates a natural-looking environment and helps maintain humidity for moisture-loving reptiles. Deco-logs and Hiding Places offer security and rough textures to aid in shedding.

Cascading Creek Viquarium

Water's Edge Viquarium

Care Guide to 25 Common Reptiles

Reptile	Terrarium Specs.	Heat	Diet and Care	Diet Supplements	Special Comments
1) Agama *Agama agama ssp.*	Large area—use Hiding Places and Critter Logs.	Sizzle Stones. A tropical lizard; enjoys basking.	Insects and some fruit. Heat up to 86°F.	Vitalife and Reptical as directed. Young need small insects.	Very territorial; males tend to fight. Requires dry, high heat.
2) Green Anole *Anolis carolinensis*	Arboreal lizard—Tree Flora: needs branches for climbing. Evergreen Moss for humidity, tall cage.	Sizzle Stones—Regular or Junior depending on number of Anoles kept.	Flies, insects, and spiders, some fruit. Heat 75°F–80°F.	Vitalife as directed. Young prefer summer locations. Vitafly good substitute.	Males may fight. Males larger than females, with large pink dewlap. Prefers drinking droplets.
3) Northern Alligator Lizard, *Gerrhonotus coeruleus ssp.*	Terrestrial—moderate size with Hiding Places and Critter Logs.	Normal room temperature, with Sizzle Stones or Tropical Hot Block.	Insects, spiders, millipeds, and snails. Heat 65°F–75°F.	Vitalife and Reptical as directed.	Prefers cooler climates. Needs some humidity.
4) Blue-Tongued Skink *Tiliqua gigas*	Terrestrial—needs large area.	Super Sizzle Stones or Super Hot Block.	Canned dog food, insects, berries, fruit, and some small vertebrates. Heat 70°F–85°F.	Vitalife and Reptical a must due to rapid body growth. May take Aquatic Turtle Food.	Thrives in captivity. May reach 24" in length. Bright blue tongue.
5) Five-Lined Skink *Eumeces fasciatus*	Terrestrial—moderate size with Hiding Places; prefers bark flooring.	Sizzle Stones.	Insects, larvae, spiders, and earthworms. Heat 70°F–85°F.	Vitalife, Reptical as directed. May take Vitafly.	Young have vivid stripes and bright blue tail.
6) Green Iguana *Iguana iguana ssp.* (photo p. 3)	Large area necessary. Adults mostly arboreal; larger Hiding Places; needs water for bathing.	Sizzle Stones a must.	Herbivorous—fruits, berries, vegetables, some insects taken. Heat 80°F–95°F.	Vitalife and Reptical as directed. Land Turtle Food preferred by many.	Young tend to be mostly terrestrial. May reach lengths of up to 5'–6'. Prefers tropical, humid environment. Belly heat essential for digestion.
7) Knight Anole *Anolis equestris ssp.* (photo p. 50)	Mostly arboreal. Requires more space than *A. carolinensis.* Average adult size is 12". Tetra Flora.	Sizzle Stones or Hot Block.	Insects, flies, spiders—adults may take "pinkies." Heat 75°F–80°F.	Vitalife and Reptical as directed. Vitafly.	Very fearful of snakes. Relatively slow-moving, with strong jaws.
8) Thai Water Dragon *Physignathus cocincinus*	Large area necessary with ample water for bathing. Needs Hiding Places.	Super Sizzle Stones or Super Hot Block.	Carnivorous—also insects and some fruit. Heat 77°F–85°F.	Vitalife as directed. Reptical as needed. May take Land and Aquatic Turtle Food.	Prefers locations near water; enjoys bathing frequently.
9) Leopard Gecko *Eublepharus macularius* (photo p. 54)	Moderate size. Hiding Places, Critter Logs, and Evergreen Moss for local moisture.	Sizzle Stones or Tropical Hot Block.	Insects, flies, spiders. Heat 75°F–85°F (cooler at night).	Vitalife as directed. May take Vitafly.	Males territorial and may fight. Does well in captivity. Requires dry conditions.
10) Boa Constrictor *Boa constrictor ssp.*	Partly arboreal. Tall cage with limbs for climbing. Adults require larger space.	Regular Sizzle Stones to Super Sizzle Stones depending on size of snake.	Rodents—may take rabbits or chickens. Heat 77°F–85°F.	Vitalife and Reptical both essential for growth.	May attain length of 12'–13'. Young require dry, warm environment to prevent respiratory problems.
11) Glossy Snake *Arizona elegans ssp.*	Moderate size, rectangular cage. Prefers sand. Hiding Places and Critter Logs.	Sizzle Stones or Desert Hot Block.	Carnivorous—prefers lizards but may take small mice. Heat 78°F–85°F (cooler at night).	Vitalife as directed.	Will burrow. Requires hot, dry conditions. May live 12 years in captivity.
12) Indian Python *Python molurus ssp.*	Large area. Hiding Places, rectangular cage.	Sizzle Stones or Hot Block.	Rodents and larger mammals, possibly chickens. Heat 77°F–86°F.	Vitalife and Reptical essential for growth.	Thrives in captivity but may attain 20' in length and proper housing must be provided.
13) Indigo Snakes and Cribos *Drymarchon corais ssp.*	Needs ample space, many Hiding Places, Tree Flora.	Super Sizzle Stones or Super Hot Block.	Frogs, small mammals, birds, other snakes, lizards, and young turtles. Heat 75°F–85°F.	Vitalife and Reptical as directed.	A large colubrine, up to 9' in length. Long-lived in captivity. Eats other snakes.

Care Guide to 25 Common Reptiles

Reptile	Terrarium Specs.	Heat	Diet and Care	Diet Supplements	Special Comments
14) Green Tree Python *Chondropython viridis*	Highly arboreal; requires tall vivarium with horizontal branches.	Sizzle Stones with bottom or overhead light.	Rats, mice, and other warm-blooded food. Heat 77°F–88°F.	Vitalife as directed.	Young are brick red, yellow, or chocolate; adults are bright green. Protected in the wild. Not to be confused with Emerald Boa (*Corallus caninus*).
15) Bull Snake *Pituophis melanoleucus* ssp.	Moderate size, rectangular shape. Hiding Places, Critter Logs for juveniles, Tree Flora.	Sizzle Stones or Hot Block.	Mostly mice or small rats. Heat 75°F–85°F.	Vitalife as directed.	Known also as Pine or Gopher Snakes. Many subspecies. Some mistaken for rattlesnakes, since they vibrate their tails, hiss, and strike when first approached.
16) Garter Snake *Thamnophis sirtalis* ssp.	Moderate size, rectangular shape. Hiding Places, Critter Logs, Tree Flora, and Evergreen Moss.	Sizzle Stones or Hot Block. Must provide some dry areas.	Amphibians, fish, and earthworms, depending on species. Heat 70°F–80°F.	Vitalife is a necessity. Cage with fish eaters.	Many species and subspecies with various markings, patterns, and color combinations. Enjoys moist environment.
17) King Snake *Lampropeltis getulus* ssp.	Needs roomy cage with many Hiding Places. Rarely climbs.	Sizzle Stones or Hot Block, size depending on species kept.	Mice, lizards, birds, eggs, and other snakes. Heat 75°F–85°F.	Vitalife and Reptical as directed.	Do not house large and small specimens together, since one may become a meal for the other. Common subspecies are the Eastern, California, Florida, and Speckled. Record longevity exceeds 24 years. Easy to care for.
18) Smooth Green Snake *Opheodrys vernalis* ssp.	Moderate size. Hiding Places, Critter Logs, Tree Flora. Mostly terrestrial but a good climber.	Sizzle Stones or Tropical Hot Block.	Insects and spiders, grasshoppers and caterpillars. Heat 68°F–80°F (cooler at night).	Vitalife as directed. May also take Vitalfy.	Prefers mixture of Hiding Places, tree limbs, logs where it actively chases food. Rough Green Snake (*O. aestivus*) treated same except more arboreal.
19) Corn Snake *Elaphe guttata* ssp.	Moderate size, rectangular shape. Hiding Places and Tree Flora.	Sizzle Stones or Hot Block.	Mice, rats, birds, and bats. Heat 75°F–85°F.	Vitalife as directed.	Does well in captivity. Excellent beginner snake. Attractive coloration. An expert climber. Record in captivity, over 21 years.
20) Mud Turtle *Kinosternon subrubrum* ssp.	Requires shallow water with moderate room. Must have dry basking area. Hiding Places.	Sizzle Stones or Hot Block in dry area.	Entirely carnivorous. Insects, worms, and meats. Heat 70°F–80°F.	Vitalife as directed. Reptical as juvenile.	Surprisingly terrestrial. Usually keeps to muddy bottoms of slow-moving fresh or brackish water. Easy to maintain and lives many years in captivity.
21) Wood Turtle *Clemmys insculpta* (photo p. 38)	Large area. Plenty of water available with easy access. Hiding Places and wood chips.	Regular Sizzle Stones or Tropical Hot Block.	Worms, slugs, insects, fruits, tadpoles, and various plant material. Heat 65°F–75°F.	Vitalife as directed. Reptical an essential part of the diet. Vitalfy as directed.	Mostly terrestrial. Skin of neck and forelegs usually reddish orange. Excellent climber. Reputation for being intelligent.
22) Spiny Soft-Shelled Turtle *Trionyx spiniferus* ssp.	Aquatic environment. Dry basking area needed. Prefers muddy bottom, shallow water.	Tropical Hot Block or Super Hot Block in dry basking area.	Fish, frogs, insects, and tadpoles, various meats. Heat 77°F–86°F.	Vitalife and Reptical as directed. Vitalfy readily taken.	Basking area must be smooth or abrasions will occur on plastron. Diversify diet. Small amount of salt in water helps prevent fungus.
23) Box Turtle *Terrapene carolina* ssp.	Large area. Shallow water available. Hiding Places. May be housed outdoors also.	Sizzle Stones or Hot Block.	Slugs, earthworms, insects, fruit, strawberries, and mushrooms. Canned dog food taken. Heat 75°F–85°F.	Vitalife as directed. Reptical while juvenile. Vitalfy as directed.	A few have lived more than 100 years. Fond of occasional misting. Various markings among species. Males usually have red eyes.
24) Pond Slider *Trachemys scripta* ssp.	Plenty of water. Approximately ⅓ dry area for basking. Underwater retreat and filtration. Hiding Places.	See chapter "Turtle Aquarium."	See chapter "Turtle Aquarium."	Vitalife as directed. Reptical essential part of diet as juvenile. Vitalfy as additional treat.	Very fond of basking. Vitamin D, calcium, phosphorus essential in diet of young to prevent soft and deformed shells. Common subspecies known as Red-Eared and Yellow-Bellied. Bright shell color tends to fade with age.
25) Painted Turtle *Chrysemys picta* ssp. (photo p. 22)	Plenty of water, as with Pond Slider. Easy access in and out of water. Hiding Places.	See chapter "Turtle Aquarium."	See chapter "Turtle Aquarium."	Vitalife as directed. Reptical essential part of diet as juvenile. Vitalfy as additional treat.	Young turtles basically carnivorous but become herbivorous as they mature. Most widespread turtle in North America and one of the prettiest. Common subspecies are Eastern, Midland, Southern, and Western.

75

Additional Reading

The study of herpetology, the science pertaining to reptiles and amphibians, is a rapidly expanding field. New publications, both specific and general, pertaining to the identification, field biology, or captive husbandry of these interesting creatures currently number several a month.

There are a number that I would like to recommend.

Easy Reading (General Herpetology)

Bartlett, Richard D., 1987. *In Search of Reptiles and Amphibians*. New York and Leiden, Netherlands: E. J. Brill.

Kauffeld, C., 1957. *Snakes and Snake Hunting*. Garden City, N.Y.: Hanover House.

————, 1969. *Snakes: The Keeper and the Kept*. Garden City, N.Y.: Doubleday.

Mehrtens, John M., 1987. *Living Snakes of the World in Color*. New York: Sterling.

Obst, Fritz J., Klaus Richter, and Udo Jacob, 1988. *The Completely Illustrated Atlas of Reptiles and Amphibians for the Terrarium*. Neptune City, N.J.: TFH.

Field Identification, U.S.A.

Behler, John L., and F. Wayne King, 1979. *The Audubon Society Field Guide to North American Reptiles and Amphibians*. New York: Knopf.

Conant, Roger, 1975. *A Field Guide to Reptiles and Amphibians of Eastern and Central North America* (revised). Boston: Houghton Mifflin.

Stebbins, Robert, 1985. *A Field Guide to Western Reptiles and Amphibians* (revised). Boston: Houghton Mifflin.

Field Identification, Worldwide

Arnold, E. N., and J. A. Burton, 1978. *A Field Guide to the Reptiles and Amphibians of Britain and Europe*. London: Collins.

Cogger, Harold G., 1979. *Reptiles and Amphibians of Australia* (revised). Sanibel, Fla.: Ralph Curtis Publishing.

Patterson, Rod, and Anthony Bannister, 1987. *Reptiles of Southern Africa*. Cape Town, South Africa: Struik.

Husbandry

Alderton, David, 1986. *A Petkeeper's Guide to Reptiles and Amphibians*. Morris Plains, N.J.: Tetra Press.

Coburn, John, 1987. *Snakes & Lizards, Their Care and Breeding in Captivity*. Sanibel, Fla.: Ralph Curtis Publishing.

Mattison, Chris, 1982. *The Care of Reptiles and Amphibians in Captivity*. Poole, Dorset, England: Blandford.

Zimmerman, Elke, 1983. *Breeding Terrarium Animals*. Neptune City, N.J.: TFH.

Periodicals

Notes from NOAH. A monthly newsletter published by the Northern Ohio Association of Herpetologists, Department of Biology, Case Western Reserve University, Cleveland, Ohio 44106.

The Vivarium. A captive care and informational quarterly published by The American Federation of Herpetoculturists, P.O. Box 1131, Lakeside, Calif. 92040.

Herpetological Review. A more advanced quarterly which includes, among other topics, field notes, captive care, meeting notices, and book reviews. Published by the Society for the Study of Amphibians and Reptiles, Department of Zoological and Biomedical Sciences, Ohio University, Athens, Ohio 45701.

The Herptile. A quarterly devoted to field notes and captive care. Published by the International Herpetological Society, c/o Mr. David Blatchford, Bungalow No. 2, Kirkhill Cottages, St. Quivox, Ayr, Ayrshire, KA6 5HJ, Scotland.

Index

Tetra Terrafauna, a division of Tetra, is one of the world's largest providers of products and information devoted to herptiles. Please contact Tetra Terrafauna and the following address or visit us on the web at www.tetra-fish.com.

Tetra Terrafauna
3001 Commerce St.
Blacksburg, VA 24060

(800) 526-0650